Captain
James Cook

WILLIAM W. LACE

GREAT EXPLORERS

Jacques Cartier

James Cook

Hernán Cortés

Sir Francis Drake

Vasco da Gama

Sir Edmund Hillary

Robert de La Salle

Lewis and Clark

Ferdinand Magellan

Sir Ernest Shackleton

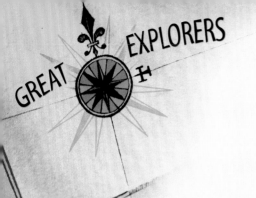

GREAT EXPLORERS

Captain James Cook

WILLIAM W. LACE

CHELSEA HOUSE
PUBLISHERS
An imprint of Infobase Publishing

GREAT EXPLORERS: CAPTAIN JAMES COOK

Chelsea House
An imprint of Infobase Publishing
132 West 31st Street
New York NY 10001

Library of Congress Cataloging-in-Publication Data
Lace, William W.
  Captain James Cook / William W. Lace.
    p. cm.
  Includes bibliographical references and index.
  ISBN 978-1-60413-416-2 (hardcover)
  1. Cook, James, 1728-1779—Travel—Juvenile literature. 2. Explorers—Great Britain—Biography—Juvenile literature. 3. Voyages around the world—Juvenile literature. 4. Oceania—Discovery and exploration—Juvenile literature. I. Title.
  G420.C65L33 2009
  910.92—dc22
  [B]   2009009891

Chelsea House books are available at special discounts when purchased in bulk quantities for businesses, associations, institutions, or sales promotions. Please call our Special Sales Department in New York at (212) 967-8800 or (800) 322-8755.

You can find Chelsea House on the World Wide Web at
http://www.chelseahouse.com

Series design by Lina Farinella
Cover design by Keith Trego

Printed in the United States of America

Bang EJB 10 9 8 7 6 5 4 3 2 1

This book is printed on acid-free paper.

All links and Web addresses were checked and verified to be correct at the time of publication. Because of the dynamic nature of the Web, some addresses and links may have changed since publication and may no longer be valid.

CONTENTS

From Farm to Sea, 1728–1768

JAMES COOK WAS ONE OF THE MOST FAMOUS AND, AT THE SAME time, the most modest of men. Although he wrote at length about the lands and seas he explored, he wrote virtually nothing about himself. He told much about the Antarctic Ice Shelf and the natives of Tahiti, yet nothing about his wife or children.

Cook sought knowledge, not fame, but the vast extent of the knowledge he provided to the world guaranteed that fame would find him. Perhaps the best measure of his accomplishments is found on maps. Three groups of islands bear his name, as well as five bays, four mountains, three reefs, three points, three towns, two channels, two rocks, and many assorted glaciers, creeks, beaches, straits, and rivers. He is the namesake of hotels and inns from New Zealand to Poland and the subject of museum exhibits from Canada to Russia.

He does not appear to have been motivated by ambition, but rather by an overwhelming curiosity to see what was on the other side of the world. It was likely this same curiosity that took him from the most humble of beginnings as the son of a

The Voyages of Captain Cook

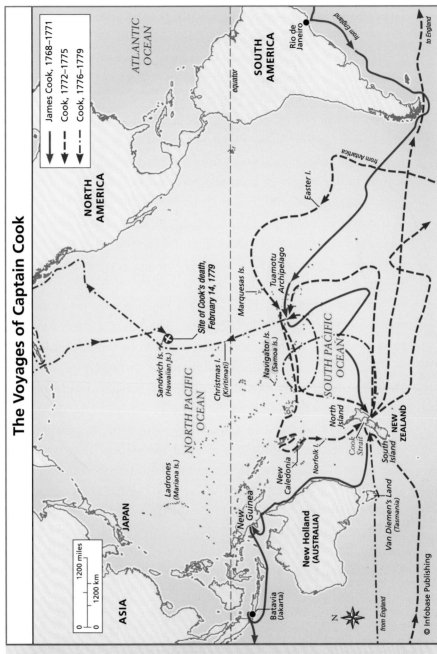

Legend:
- James Cook, 1768–1771
- Cook, 1772–1775
- Cook, 1776–1779

ATLANTIC OCEAN

NORTH AMERICA

SOUTH AMERICA

Rio de Janeiro

from England

to England

equator

from Antarctica

Easter I.

Marquesas Is.

Tuamotu Archipelago

Navigator Is. (Samoa Is.)

SOUTH PACIFIC OCEAN

Sandwich Is. (Hawaiian Is.)

Site of Cook's death, February 14, 1779

Christmas I. (Kiritimati)

NORTH PACIFIC OCEAN

Ladrones (Mariana Is.)

JAPAN

ASIA

New Guinea

New Caledonia

Norfolk I.

North Island

Cook Strait

South Island

NEW ZEALAND

New Holland (AUSTRALIA)

Van Diemen's Land (Tasmania)

from England

Batavia (Jakarta)

1200 miles

1200 km

N

© Infobase Publishing

This map shows the three exploratory voyages taken by Captain James Cook through the Pacific. Cook provided some of the most detailed information about the Pacific and was the first European to achieve contact with the eastern coastline of Australia and the Hawaiian Islands. He is also famous for the first recorded circumnavigation of New Zealand.

farm laborer in an obscure English village to an apprenticeship at a seaside grocery store to, finally, the sea itself.

Cook's father, also named James, was a native of Scotland, which occupies the northern third of the island of Great Britain. In 1707, Scotland and England united—a very unpopular move with the vast majority of the population in Scotland. The union benefited landowners, while the rest of the population was still disadvantaged. Food riots occurred in the east coast region as the effects of famine were compounded by union taxes. The population's discontent intensified when the House of Hanover succeeded to the British throne in 1714. As a result, a series of uprisings occurred, called the Jacobite Risings, that was aimed at returning King James II and VII's descendants to the throne.

It was during the First Jacobite Rebellion (1715–1716) that James Cook's father left Scotland in search of a better life. Instead of emigrating to the United States or to Canada, however, he moved only a few miles south of the United Kingdom's border to the North Yorkshire village of Marton, where he found work as a farm laborer.

He also found a wife. Grace Pace, who lived in a neighboring village, was eight years younger than Cook. They were married in 1725, and their first son, John, was born a year later. Their second son, James, was born on October 27, 1728. There would be six other children, but only James and two sisters would live beyond their twenties.

Work and School

Young James learned to work as a small boy. He did odd jobs for a local woman named Mary Walker, whose husband owned the farm where James's father occasionally worked. In exchange for his labor, Mrs. Walker taught him how to read. Later, James worked as part of a team with his father and his brother John.

They earned a high reputation for their work, and James Sr. was hired as a foreman on the estate of Thomas Skottowe, near the town of Ayton.

Skottowe was impressed, not only with young James's hard work, but also by what promised to be his keen mind. He paid for James to attend the Postgate School, a school created to educate farm workers' children. Local historian John Graves wrote in 1808, as quoted in J. C. Beaglehole's *The Life of Captain James Cook*, that Cook's qualities of perseverance and resolution "were conspicuous, even in his boyish days. . . . Cook might be seen in the midst of his comrades, strenuously contending that they should proceed to some particular spot." Still, Graves wrote, Cook had "the reverence and respect of his companions."

In the summer of 1745, when Cook was 16 years old, he moved 20 miles away to the seaside fishing village of Staithes. He served as an apprentice in the grocery/clothing business of William Sanderson. After working for Sanderson for 18 months, Cook knew two things: He did not want to be a shop-keeper, and he did want to go to sea.

Although he was disappointed to lose a reliable employee, Sanderson agreed to help Cook. Sanderson took him to nearby Whitby and arranged a formal apprenticeship to shipowners John and Henry Walker. The Walkers were Quakers (a Christian movement that started in England in the mid-seventeenth century) who were in the coal trade business. Cook would work for room, board, and a small wage for three years, and the Walkers would teach him seamanship.

To the young man, who was only a few months removed from the village of Marton, Whitby must have seemed huge. At the time that Cook lived there, it had about 10,000 residents and was a large trading port. Home to more than 200 ships that carried English goods to ports as distant as America and India, it was also a center for shipbuilding.

Hauling Coal

The Industrial Revolution was just beginning in Great Britain. The fuel of that revolution was coal. More than 1,000 ships carried coal down the coast of England and across the North Sea. More than a million tons were needed each year to fill the factory furnaces and stoves of London alone.

The preferred vessel for hauling coal and the one used by the Walkers was the Whitby collier, commonly called a "cat." As quoted by Beaglehole, it was distinguished by "a narrow stern, projecting quarters, a deep waist, and by having no ornamental figure on the prow." In other words, it was squat and unattractive but could navigate shallow waters and carry huge amounts of cargo.

Colliers would make up to 10 round-trips in a year, taking on coal at Newcastle, which was north of Whitby, and working their way down the coast and then up the Thames River to London. Cook began making such journeys in February 1747, on the *Freelove*. In addition to the captain (master), there was a mate, or second-in-command, plus a cook; a carpenter; five "AB," or able-bodied seamen; and ten "servants," or apprentices. Cook, at age 18, was one of the oldest apprentices.

He stayed with the *Freelove* until June 1748, at which time he was assigned to a new coal ship, the *Three Brothers*. John Jefferson, the captain of the *Freelove*, held the same office on the new collier, and the fact that he took Cook with him may have been an indication of his opinion of the apprentice's progress. The *Three Brothers* was larger than the *Freelove* and made trips to Ireland and to Liverpool, a city on the western coast of England.

In December 1749, Cook completed his three-year apprenticeship. In April 1750, he signed on as a full-fledged seaman on the *Three Brothers*, which was headed to Norway. In 1752, he moved to another Walker vessel, the *Friendship*, as mate under Robert Watson, who had been mate on the *Freelove* when Cook began his service.

Cook served as mate of the *Friendship* for three years, gaining in skill as a sailor and in knowledge as a navigator. He had earned the confidence and respect of the Walkers and, in the spring of 1755, he was offered a position as officer in

In 1755, Cook joined the Royal Navy as an able seaman on the H.M.S. *Eagle*. He quickly moved up the ranks. Within a month, Cook was promoted to master's mate. Two years later, he was promoted again to the rank of master.

charge of navigation on the *Friendship*. It was a remarkable achievement, coming only nine years after he had begun his apprenticeship, but Cook turned it down. Instead, he enlisted in the Royal Navy, sensing a war was approaching. Great Britain entered what was later called the Seven Years' War in 1756. Although enlisting in the navy meant starting at the bottom again, Cook recognized that his career would advance more quickly in the military.

In the Navy

On June 17, 1755, Cook was assigned to the H.M.S. *Eagle* under Captain Joseph Hamar. They were to patrol the waters south of Ireland and capture French ships. Hamar did not think his crew was up for the job. Many of the new hands had been "pressed" (virtually kidnapped and forcibly enlisted), or they had been offered a choice between the navy and a jail sentence. A prize recruit like Cook was rare, and in less than a month he was promoted to master's mate. Unlike the merchant service, the master was not considered the captain, nor was he even an officer. Instead, the master was the officer in charge of navigation and the daily details of running a ship.

The *Eagle* had been on patrol only a short time when it was caught in a storm. Captain Hamar, thinking his mainmast (the chief pole that supports the sails) was cracked, came into Plymouth (located about 190 miles southwest of London) for repairs. The mast makers were unable to find anything wrong, however, and the captain was ordered to return to sea. Instead, Hamar decided to have the ship's bottom cleaned. His superiors were displeased and Hamar was relieved of his command. On October 1, Hugh Palliser was brought on as captain.

Palliser immediately recognized Cook's abilities. He began instructing Cook not only in navigation and seamanship, but also in surveying and in the charting of coastlines and bodies of water. Palliser would prove to be one of Cook's most influential supporters throughout his career.

Palliser got the *Eagle* back into service as quickly as possible, and Cook saw his first action on November 15. Patrolling the western entrance to the English Channel, the *Eagle* encountered and sank the French ship *Esperance*. In a way, it was not a smart move. If the *Esperance* had been taken as a prize or captured, and had been bought by the British navy, every man on the *Eagle*'s crew would have shared in the prize money.

It would not be until May 1757 that Cook was in another battle. This time, the *Eagle* and the *Medway* combined to capture the larger French *Duc d'Aquitaine*. It was a hard fight, resulting in 90 of Cook's shipmates having been killed or wounded and about 50 Frenchmen having been killed. This time, Cook received prize money and a promotion to the rank of master. This was remarkable since, at this point, Cook had served only two years in the navy.

To Canada

Cook served as master of the H.M.S. *Pembroke* as it headed to Canada. Whoever controlled the French fort in Louisburg on the Gulf of Saint Lawrence in Canada and the city of Quebec on the Saint Lawrence River, would determine the direction of the war, because capturing them would negate all French possessions in North America. At that time, France's possessions included the Saint Lawrence River, the Great Lakes, and the Mississippi River. The British were determined to take control of Canada and the Ohio River Valley.

To accomplish the conquest of Canada, the British sent a fleet under the command of Admiral Edward Boscawen. Part of the fleet, which sailed from Plymouth on February 22, 1758, was Cook's *Pembroke*.

This was Cook's first long voyage, and he saw for the first time the extent to which disease decimated a crew. The men developed scurvy, a serious and often-fatal ailment caused by vitamin C deficiency due to lack of fresh fruit and vegetables. By the time the *Pembroke* reached the British port at Halifax, Nova Scotia, 26 men had died and many more had to be hospitalized. Consequently, there were not enough able-bodied men to work the ship. By the time the *Pembroke* caught up with the fleet, the battle for Louisburg already had begun.

Disease had made inroads on the French, as well. Typhus, or "ship fever," had depleted the French fleet over the past year. Thousands of sailors had died, and the intended French reinforcements never made it to Louisburg. By the time the *Pembroke* arrived, British troops had landed, and the fort was under bombardment from land and sea. On July 25, 1758, Cook took part in a major battle when small boats from the *Pembroke* and from other ships in the fleet assaulted two French warships during a fog, burning one and capturing the other. Louisburg surrendered the next day.

Learning a New Skill

Quebec, however, promised to be a harder conquest, and the British commanders feared that there was not enough time before winter to capture it. While he waited for their orders, Cook was far from idle, however. Shortly after the surrender of Louisburg, he had a chance meeting that changed the course of his life. While walking on shore, he met an army lieutenant named Samuel Holland. Holland was seated at a table, taking notes and making a drawing of the coastline.

Cook was fascinated. He had learned about charts and the mathematics that went into making them, but this was his first time actually seeing the charts created. Holland was glad to have a pupil, and he came aboard the *Pembroke* the next day in order to, as quoted by Beaglehole's *The Life of Captain James Cook*, "make him acquainted with the whole process." The captain, John Simcoe, was not only willing for Cook to learn surveying from Holland, but he wanted to learn himself. Illness prevented Simcoe from achieving this goal, but he gave permission for Cook to continue his studies with Holland and to eventually create a survey himself. This first effort, a chart of Gaspé Bay off of Quebec, Canada, was sent to the naval office and published the next year.

Cook's surveying then took a more serious turn. The Saint Lawrence River was hard to navigate in some places, especially for large ships. What few charts the British had were inaccurate, so Simcoe ordered Cook and Holland to sail up the river to take measurements and correct existing charts. They also produced a set of sailing directions with the lengthy title of "Descriptions for sailing in and out of Ports, with soundings, Marks for particular Rocks, Shoals, etc. with the Latitude, Longitude, Tides, and Variation of the Compass."

These charts and directions helped make it possible for the British fleet to safely negotiate the Saint Lawrence, but there were other difficulties. Some of the more difficult passages had been marked with buoys, but the French commander at Quebec, General Montcalm, had ordered them removed. Consequently, Cook and masters from other ships had to go ahead of the fleet in small boats, testing the depth of the water and marking the best route.

The Fight for Quebec

The fleet reached Quebec on June 27, 1759. Now, Cook had to find a way to get the troops safely ashore. His task was not without danger. One day, he was in a small boat setting out buoys when canoes full of French soldiers and their American Indian allies tried to cut him off. Cook and his crew made it to a nearby island. They jumped out of the boat just as American Indian warriors were climbing over the stern. Reinforcements arrived and the canoes were driven away.

As a young sailor in the Royal Navy, Cook took part in the siege of Quebec before the battle of the Plains of Abraham on September 13, 1759 (*above*). Cook was responsible for mapping much of the entrance to the Saint Lawrence River, allowing General Wolfe to make his famous amphibious assault. This battle eventually led to Great Britain's capture of nearly all of France's possessions in eastern North America.

The men continued to look for suitable landing places in Quebec. General Thomas Wolfe, commander of the ground forces, was on the verge of retiring for the winter. Luckily, Wolfe found a protected cove beneath a cliff called the Plains of Abraham. In the early morning darkness of September 13, Wolfe and his troops went ashore and climbed up the steep cliff, hauling their artillery with them.

In order to draw attention away from the actual landing site, boats from the *Pembroke* and several other ships set out buoys downriver to fool the French into thinking this would be the location of the main assault. The French were driven back by gunfire from the British ships, and the bombardment went on for most of the night.

The battle of the Plains of Abraham had begun. Beaglehole's *The Life of Captain James Cook* says Cook wrote in his master's log about how they "totally defeated them [and] continued the pursuit to the very gates of the city." Quebec had fallen, and Great Britain was now the dominant power in North America.

Shortly after the battle, Cook was transferred as master to the *Northumberland*. Its captain was Lord Colville, who like Palliser would turn out to have a dramatic effect on Cook's career. While much of the victorious fleet returned home, the *Northumberland* was to remain in North America another two-and-a-half years. With the fighting over, there was little for the British squadron at Halifax to do. Cook, however, continued his surveying and his studies. James King, one of his officers on a later voyage, wrote, as quoted by Beaglehole, that Cook "read Euclid [a Greek mathematician], and applied himself to the study of mathematics and astronomy, without any other assistance, than what a few books, and his own industry, afforded him."

Back in England

The *Northumberland* finally sailed for home on October 7, 1762, arriving 19 days later. Cook received his accumulated pay of £291, the equivalent today of about $45,000. Now 34 years old, Cook had been away from England for four years. His country was in a state of peace, and Cook decided it was a good time to find a wife. Less than two months later, on December 21, he married Elizabeth Batts, 13 years his junior and the daughter of an innkeeper.

In the meantime, Cook had delivered to the navy the charts and drawings he had done while on the *Northumberland*. The charts of the Saint Lawrence that he had created with Holland already had been published, but Cook's name had not been connected with them. Lord Colville, his mentor and captain of the *Northumberland,* wanted to ensure Cook received the credit he deserved. On December 30, Captain Colville wrote to the Lords of the Admiralty, commanders of the navy. According to Richard Hough's biography *Captain James Cook,* Colville told them "from my experience of Mr. Cook's genius and capacity, I think him well qualified for the work he had performed and for greater undertakings of the same kind."

Those undertakings lay back on the other side of the Atlantic. The Treaty of Paris, which ended the Seven Years' War in 1763, had given the island of Newfoundland to Great Britain. Newfoundland's governor, Thomas Graves, needed a surveyor to map out all the bays and harbors. Graves had known Cook in Halifax, and he had also heard about Cook's stellar reputation from Palliser and Colville. Graves hired Cook as a surveyor. It was the start of many long absences from Elizabeth. She was expecting their first child and knew that her husband would not be there to see it born.

In April, Cook received his first assignment. He was to survey the French islands of Saint-Pierre-et-Miquelon, islands off the coast of Newfoundland. Under the terms of the treaty, the islands were to be given back to France on the condition that they would not be fortified. While aboard the H.M.S. *Tweed,* Cook worked quickly yet accurately, and he had the maps finished by August. Hough's *Captain James Cook* notes that the *Tweed*'s captain credited the speed at which the maps had been produced to "the unwearied assiduity of Mr. Cook."

Cook reported to Graves that he needed a smaller ship to more properly navigate close to the shoreline, and one was provided. The schooner *Sally* was purchased and renamed the H.M.S. *Grenville.* Cook was assigned to survey harbors on the north shore of Newfoundland, one of which was subsequently renamed Cook's Harbour. In October, with winter setting in, Graves sent Cook back to England to finish his charts. Hough's

Captain James Cook says that Graves wrote to the Admiralty, praising Cook's "indefatigable industry" and saying that his "pains and attentions are beyond my description."

Family Life

In April, Cook settled into family life back home in East London. He had missed the birth of his first son, James, seven weeks earlier, but he was in time for the baptismal ceremony. The expanding family needed a house, and one was found on Assembly Row, a short distance away from the center of London.

Each morning, Cook and his assistant, Edward Smart, worked at the Admiralty, turning their rough drawings and observations into "fair copies" to be published. Cook was not to remain on shore for long, however. By May, he was headed back to Newfoundland, once more leaving a pregnant Elizabeth behind.

Landing in June, he quickly got back to work as a surveyor. Smart had died shortly before the sailing, so Cook had a new partner, William Parker, who later rose to the rank of admiral. Graves's term as governor ended, and he was succeeded by Cook's former mentor Captain Palliser. Cook and Parker took up the survey where it had been left off the previous year, finishing the northern coast and working their way down the long western edge of the island.

The rough charts were completed by mid-October. Cook returned to his Assembly Row home in December, just in time for the birth of his second son, Nathaniel. He resumed his work at the Admiralty and supervised the refitting of the *Grenville*, changing it from a schooner to a much more maneuverable brig.

Cook was to spend two more summers surveying the Newfoundland coast. One of the few incidents to interrupt his work occurred on August 5, 1766. Having kept up his studies of astronomy, he knew that an eclipse of the sun was to occur that day. Using his surveyor's tools, he recorded his observations and sent them to Dr. John Bevis, a physician and an astronomer who was a member of the Royal Society of London for the Improvement of Natural Knowledge, also known as the Royal Society. Dr. Bevis was impressed with the accuracy of the report, and he forwarded it to the society.

In August 1767, at the end of Cook's last surveying season in Newfoundland, Palliser wrote to the secretary of the Admiralty, as quoted by Hough in *Captain James Cook*, that the "publication of [Cook's charts], I am of opinion, will be a great encouragement to new adventurers in the fisheries upon these coasts."

A New Assignment

In April, the *Grenville* was readied once more for the voyage back to Newfoundland, but Cook would not be on board. As reported in Beaglehole's *The Life of Captain James Cook*, the minutes of an Admiralty meeting reported that Michael Lane had been appointed surveyor of Newfoundland and that the navy had decided to send a vessel "to the Southward."

This "Southward" journey had been in the making for some time. It had been only a little over 200 years since the Polish astronomer Nicolaus Copernicus had established that Earth was not the center of the universe, but one of several planets revolving around the sun. By Cook's time, astronomers were trying to map out the solar system, calculating the distance between the planetary orbits. Edmund Halley proposed in 1716 that such distances could be calculated by making observations from many points around the globe of Venus in its transits, or passages between Earth and the sun.

An international effort had been made to get such measurements in 1761, but with limited success. The next transit of Venus would take place in 1769. Scientists were anxious for their efforts to gain measurements to be successful, since another transit would not occur for another five years.

In June 1766, the Royal Society began preparing for the 1769 transit, but it took five months to form a committee and another year for the committee to actually meet. For Great Britain's participation in the multinational project, observers would be sent to three locations: Norway, Hudson Bay in Canada, and the Pacific Ocean. The society also recommended that the Pacific observation be done by Scottish geographer and fellow of the Royal Society Alexander Dalrymple.

Dalrymple, however, proved to be difficult. He was only mildly interested in astronomy. His real reason for wishing to undertake the mission was to explore the Pacific, and more specifically to try to discover Terra Australis, the mysterious southern continent first proposed by Greek philosopher Aristotle. Many scientists, including Dalrymple, firmly believed that a southern continent had to exist somewhere to balance the landmasses north of the equator.

When Dalrymple was offered the post of senior observer in the Pacific, he accepted only on the condition that he be made commander of the ship as well as in charge of the scientific work. The navy would not accept such a condition. Philip Stevens, the secretary of the Admiralty, knew Cook and admired his work. Captain Palliser also was a strong voice on Cook's behalf. On May 5, 1768, the Royal Society offered the job of commander and principal observer to Cook. After 10 years of sailing across the Atlantic, Cook was about to go to the other side of the world.

The
First Voyage,
1768–1771

On August 26, 1768, the *Endeavour* sailed from Plymouth. It would be away for almost three years. The 85 men packed on board the 197-foot ship would experience everything from snow at the southern tip of South America to tropical breezes at the island of Tahiti. They also would battle everything from shipwreck to disease. Their primary mission, the observation of Venus, would prove disappointing, but their discoveries would add enormously to humankind's knowledge of the planet they inhabited.

There had been much to do between Cook's appointment in May and their scheduled departure in August. The ship chosen by the Admiralty could not have been more to his liking: a Whitby-built "cat" similar to those in which he had transported coal years earlier. Its name had been changed from the *Earl of Pembroke* to something more suitable for the mission: the *Endeavour*.

As captain of the *Endeavour*, although his official naval rank was lieutenant, Cook had considerable say in the selection of his officers and crew. Navigator Samuel Wallis had recently returned from a voyage around the world and had discovered the island of Tahiti, which he named King George's Island. Several members of Wallis's crew, including Third Lieutenant John Gore, Master Robert Molyneux, and Warrant Officers Dick Pickersgill and Francis Wilkinson, signed on with Cook. Cook's second-in-command was Charles Clerke, and the surgeon was William Monkhouse, whose brother Jonathan joined as a midshipman. Sergeant John Edgcumbe headed a group of 12 marines.

The Civilians

The selection of the civilians on board was largely up to the Admiralty and the Royal Society. Joseph Banks was the leader of the scientific contingent. He could not have been more different from Cook. Unlike Cook, Banks was raised in a privileged family. In school, he was not a serious student until he became interested in botany. Indeed, he was much more interested in the plants he would discover on the voyage than on observations of Venus. Yet, he was appointed to the *Endeavour* through his friendship with the First Lord of the Admiralty, Lord Sandwich. He brought with him four personal servants and two greyhounds.

The only true astronomer on board was Charles Green. The rest of the civilians were there to support Banks's botanical interests. There was fellow botanist Daniel Solander, artists Sydney Parkinson and Alexander Buchan, and secretary Herman Spöring.

Cook was busy through the early summer, traveling almost daily between his London home and the Thames River port of Deptford. In Deptford, and later in Plymouth after a trial run, he supervised the fitting-out of the *Endeavour* and the purchase and loading of supplies. The list of necessities included everything from weapons and tools to the immense quantities of food and drink that would be needed: 4 tons of beer, 185 pounds of cheese, tons of salt beef and hard biscuits, and as much fresh meat, fruits, and vegetables as could be expected not to spoil. In addition, there were live pigs, steers, poultry, and a goat to furnish milk for the officers.

There were also hundreds of pounds of portable soup—a dehydrated meat product to which water would be added—and a large quantity of sauerkraut. The sauerkraut had proven to help prevent scurvy. Cook's voyages would be largely free of this disease, mainly because of his insistence on having sauerkraut as a regular part of the crew's diet. Most of the sailors hated it, but they ate it anyway, rather than receive lashings.

The *Endeavour* was ready to sail on August 20. Cook had gathered the crew and, as was required, read to them the navy's Articles of War—the laws under which they would live. Hough's *Captain James Cook* says he recorded in his log that the men "were well satisfied and expressed great cheerfulness and readiness to prosecute our voyage."

The Voyage Begins

The voyage would be delayed for an additional six days because of adverse winds. When the *Endeavour* finally sailed on August 26, 1768, the weather was so foul that Joseph Banks was seasick for almost a week. One small boat washed overboard, as did three or four dozen fowl.

The high winds, however, meant swift sailing, and it took only 10 days for the *Endeavour* to reach its first stop, the island of Madeira, located about 400 miles off the northwestern coast of Africa. Here, Banks and his colleagues went ashore to study the local plants while Cook supervised the loading of more supplies, including almost 4,000 pounds of onions and 3,000 gallons of wine.

The rest of the voyage across the Atlantic was mostly uneventful. The *Endeavour* pulled into the harbor at Rio de Janeiro, Brazil, in South America, on November 12 (see map on page 7). Banks and his colleagues spent some time ashore

Botanist Joseph Banks has approximately 80 species of plants named after him. On Cook's first voyage of discovery to the south Pacific Ocean, Banks made the first scientific description of the bougainvillea garden plant and made the first major collection of Australian flora, describing many species new to science.

studying plants, and Cook was able to buy more supplies through a Portuguese agent.

They continued to make their way down the South American coast. The weather grew steadily colder, and the crew donned thick jackets known as fearnoughts. In early January 1769, the *Endeavour* reached Tierra del Fuego, a group of islands at the southern tip of South America, and prepared to round Cape Horn.

At this time, the only known route between the Atlantic and Pacific oceans had been the dangerous Strait of Magellan, discovered by Portuguese explorer Francisco Magellan in 1519. It was generally thought that the land to the south of the strait was part of a great unexplored southern continent, Terra Australis. Not until 1575 did the English explorer Francis Drake find that there was open sea south of the tip of South America.

IN PRAISE OF SAUERKRAUT

Scurvy, a disease brought on by a deficiency of vitamin C, was common among sailors, pirates, and soldiers. It customarily caused numerous deaths on long sea voyages and even played a large role in World War I. It is believed that ancient Greek physician Hippocrates was the first to observe the disease. In the thirteenth century, the Crusaders frequently suffered from it. In 1614, John Woodall, surgeon general of the East India Company, wrote about scurvy in a book, where he recommended fresh foods to be the cure for the disease.

Dutch sailors were the first to discover that the pickled cabbage known as sauerkraut was useful in preventing scurvy. James Cook was the first captain, however, to keep his ships almost scurvy-free, some believe due to his insistence on including sauerkraut in the diet. It was the only vegetable that retained a reasonable amount of ascorbic acid, or vitamin C, in a pickled state. In his first-voyage journal, he described one way he got his sailors to eat it.

The sauerkraut the men at first would not eat until I put in practice a method I never once knew to fail with seamen, and this was

Instead of circling the entire group of islands at the cape, Cook chose a shortcut through the Strait of Le Maire. It took two days of battling adverse currents and winds. Then, before rounding the cape itself, he decided to dock at Success Bay to gather fresh water and wood.

On January 21, the *Endeavour* set sail. Four days later, the crew sighted the tall bluff that marked Horn Island. The *Endeavour* swung well to the south, taking advantage of unusually calm waters. Within another week, they were in the Pacific Ocean headed northwest. As the weeks went by, the weather grew warmer, and the fearnoughts went back into storage. The men began to look forward to Tahiti, no doubt encouraged by

to have some of it dress'd [served] every day for the cabin table, and permitted all the officers without exception to make use of it and left it to the option of the men either to take as much as they pleased or none at all; but this practice was not continued above a week before I found it necessary to put every one on board to an allowance, for such are the tempers and dispositions of seamen in general that whatever you give them out of the common way, although it be ever so much for their good yet it will not go down with them and you will hear nothing but murmuring against the man that first invented it; but the moment they see their superiors set a value upon it, it becomes the finest stuff in the world and the inventor a damned honest fellow.

Historians now believe Cook's most effective methods for keeping his men healthy were his frequent replenishing of fresh foods, his enforcement of cleanliness, and his ban against the consumption of fat scrubbed from the ship's copper pans (the fat would acquire substances from the hot copper that irritated the gut and prevented the absorption of vitamins).

Today, scurvy is rarely seen among adults in modern Western society, although infants and the elderly are sometimes affected. Scurvy is still widespread in poor areas, where the population is dependent upon external food aid and has poor dietary choices.

their shipmates who had sailed with Wallis two years before. They had heard stories of the mild climate, the plentiful food, and the attractive women.

The Tahitians

On April 10, the tall mountains of Tahiti were barely visible. Three days later, the ship dropped anchor in Matavai Bay. The *Endeavour* was quickly surrounded by canoes, and the natives began to trade with the crew, handing over food in exchange for beads and trinkets. After a time, Cook and some of the other sailors went ashore and were warmly greeted by the large crowd.

According to Hough's *Captain James Cook*, artist Sydney Parkinson, who had been hired by Banks to draw the plants they found, wrote in his journal:

> The people in the canoes were of a pale, tawny complexion and had long, black hair. They seemed to be very good natured, and not of a covetous [greedy] disposition; giving us a couple of cocoa nuts, or a basket of apples, for a button or a nail.

He would soon change his mind. The same day, as he was trading with some of the people in one area of the ship, another "pilfered an earthen vessel out of my cabin." In the next day's journal entry, he described the natives as "attempting to steal everything they could get their hands on." The Europeans were to learn that the Tahitians' notions of property and ownership were very different from theirs. Stealing was rampant, and often the thieves, when confronted, would hand back the stolen articles and carry on as if nothing had happened.

Their differences were emphasized when, during a feast on shore, Botanist Daniel Solander and Dr. William Monkhouse had their pockets picked. When Banks went to their host, a chief nicknamed Hercules, and demanded that the goods be

On January 15, 1769, the *Endeavor* reached the Bay of Good Success in Tierra del Fuego (*above*). Cook and several of his men disembarked to look for new species of plants and animals. Although it was summer (January is a summer month south of the equator), it was bitterly cold and the men found themselves lost in a snowstorm. Two men froze to death after being separated from the rest of the party.

returned, the leader was puzzled. He offered as repayment their choice from a pile of cloth. When this was angrily refused, Hercules went off to find the thief and then returned the goods.

After a few days, the *Endeavour* crew got down to business. Cook selected a piece of open land at one end of the bay as an ideal spot to set up his instruments to measure the transit of Venus. On April 15, he went ashore with part of the crew to take possession of the site, which he named Point Venus, and to set out the measurements for a fort. He had decided that the instruments and their users had to have protection from would-be thieves and invaders from another island.

His work at Point Venus did not get off to a good start. Cook drew a long line in the sand and indicated to the locals that they should never cross it. Then, he set out to do some trading, leaving Midshipman Jonathan Monkhouse with the marines as guards. A few minutes later, Cook heard musket fire and ran back to the site. He found that one of the natives had run across the line, had knocked down one of the marines, and had stolen his musket. Monkhouse had then ordered his men to open fire, killing the thief and wounding several others. It was only with difficulty that peace was restored.

The Fort at Point Venus

A few days later, the crew began building the fort. On three sides (the fourth was a riverbank), they erected a wall of earth and sand with a palisade of tree trunks on top, their upper ends sharpened into points. They built ramparts, or raised platforms, at points along the palisade and mounted cannons borrowed from the ship. Inside the fort was a self-contained community complete with living quarters, a kitchen, food storage, storage for gunpowder and shot, and even a blacksmith. The locals, although mystified by the fort's purpose, eagerly helped in cutting and hauling the trees.

Thanks to the industry of Cook's men and the relatively swift passage they had made from England, everything was ready for the observation of Venus six weeks before it was to take place. This was not entirely good news, for it meant weeks of comparative leisure for the crew, and sailors at leisure were bound to get into trouble sooner or later.

The men who had sailed with Wallis had told lurid stories about the island women, and Cook wrote in his journal that "the women were so very liberal with their favours." This did not mean, however, that the women were totally without morals; rather, they viewed sex as a commodity to be used in trade. This casual attitude toward sex was a source of amazement to their visitors. Parkinson wrote in his journal: ". . . What is a sin in Europe, is only a simple innocent gratification in [the South Pacific]; which is to suppose that the obligation to chastity is local, and restricted only to particular parts of the globe."

Such practices did not extend to all women. Those of the ruling classes turned down all offers. There were plenty of others, however, who were more than willing, and what they desired most in exchange for sex were metal objects. Iron was practically unknown on the island, and goods such as axes, hammers, and nails were highly prized.

This became a major problem. More than 120 pounds of nails were stolen by Cook's men from the ship's store. Cook tried to stop such pilfering by issuing severe penalties for stealing. Archibald Wolf was caught with a large quantity of nails, but he refused to name his accomplices and received two dozen lashes.

Not all the sexual liaisons were of a business nature. Parkinson, as quoted by Hough, wrote that "Most of our ship's company procured temporary wives amongst the natives." Such arrangements were based on affection rather than commerce, so much so that shortly before the end of the *Endeavour*'s stay in Tahiti, two marines attempted to desert, taking refuge in the hills with their women, only to be caught and returned.

Observations of Venus

Before that departure, however, there were still the observations of Venus to be made. On June 3, 1769, the day of the transit, Cook ordered the telescopes and other instruments to be brought from the ship and set up, not only at Point Venus, but also at two other locations in case a stray cloud should block the view from the primary site.

The clouds, however, were on Venus instead of Earth. Cook wrote in his journal that there was "an atmosphere or dusky cloud round the body of the planet." As a result, the separate observations "differed from each other . . . much more than might have been expected." As it turned out, none of the observations from around the world proved accurate enough to calculate the distance between planets.

His work in Tahiti accomplished, Cook wrote that he wanted to "leave the place as soon as possible," but it would be six weeks before the ship could be made ready. Never one to be idle, Cook took advantage of the time by sailing completely around the island in one of the ship's boats, charting the coastline.

The *Endeavour* and its crew sailed on July 13, with the natives bidding them a tearful good-bye from the shore. Many had begged Cook to take them with him, but only two were chosen. One was a boy named Tiata, whom Banks had taken on as a servant. The other was Tupaia, a young priest who had served one of the island's queens. Tupaia had more or less attached himself to Banks and promised to be of value to Cook, who wrote that he had a thorough knowledge of the geography of the South Pacific and its people and thus "was the likeliest person to answer our purpose" as a guide and interpreter.

Tupaia's skills were quickly put to use as Cook visited Raiatea, Huahine, and some of Tahiti's other island neighbors. Cook named the group the Society Islands, not because of the friendliness of their inhabitants, but because of their nearness to one another.

Cook's instructions from the Admiralty had been, once the observations of Venus were done, to sail south to latitude 40 degrees—roughly parallel with the southmost tip of present-day Australia—to seek any evidence of Terra Australis. Cook doubted that the southern continent existed, especially after his route from Cape Horn to Tahiti had gone through part of where Dalrymple had claimed it to be. Still, he was required to follow orders. He sailed about 1,500 miles south, found nothing, and decided to sail on.

Cook's instructions had said that, if no continent were discovered, he was to find and chart New Zealand, discovered in 1642 by Dutch explorer Abel Tasman. Tasman never went ashore and had been content to sail only partway along the west coast. No Europeans had been there since.

New Zealand

On October 7, after five weeks of sailing, the surgeon's attendant, Nicholas Young, spotted land to the northwest. Banks and some others were convinced they had found the Terra Australis, but Cook found that the ship's position was similar to that recorded by Tasman. The *Endeavour* had arrived at New Zealand's North Island.

Cook knew that the reason Tasman had not landed was the warlike nature of the inhabitants, the Maoris. When Cook and his men went ashore in two boats, the Maoris initially retreated into the woods, but later they advanced as if to attack. They stopped only when one was killed.

Things did not get better on the second day. The initial meeting was friendly, but when a Maori man snatched a sword from one of Cook's men and tried to escape, the sailor shot the Maori dead. Later, Cook would attempt a further landing but was attacked by Maoris in canoes. The Europeans, firing in self-defense, killed or wounded three Maoris in the process. Cook decided that the best way to convince the Maoris of his good intentions was to forcibly take a small number onto the *Endeavour* and have Tupaia, the young Tahitian priest, talk to them. He succeeded in capturing three boys and offered them food and drink. They soon overcame their fear and were taken back to shore where their armed kinsmen were waiting.

Cook was disturbed by the killings that had taken place, and on the following morning the *Endeavour* sailed. He had intended to name the bay after the ship, but he changed his mind, writing in his journal that he had named it Poverty Bay "because it afforded us no one thing we wanted."

He sailed south, hoping to have better luck, but he could not find a suitable harbor and, at the point he named Cape Turnagain, he reversed course. Passing Poverty Bay, he found anchorage in Tologa Bay. The Maoris here were friendlier, and the *Endeavour* was able to take on food and water. Still, even though some trading took place between the sailors and the Maoris, there were some violent events, such as when John Gore shot and killed a man who had traded his cloak only to snatch it back at the last minute and try to flee.

Cook now set out for the northernmost portion of New Zealand, which Tasman had reached from the western side. In mid-October, the *Endeavour* rounded East Cape and in mid-December went around North Cape. On January 11, 1770, he rounded a cape on which sat a tall mountain. He named both after the earl of Egmont, a former First Lord of the Admiralty.

Queen Charlotte's Sound

The coastline now veered southeast, but Cook continued south until he reached the northern tip of what he would ultimately prove to be New Zealand's South Island. Turning east, he passed Golden Bay—where some of Tasman's men had been killed—and Tasman Bay before finding a near-perfect harbor that he named Queen Charlotte's Sound after King George's wife.

Here, while the *Endeavour*'s hull was being repaired due to a leak, Cook made one of his most important discoveries. He had suspected that what he had been sailing around was an island and that he was now in a strait leading from one side to the other. On January 22, he took a telescope and climbed

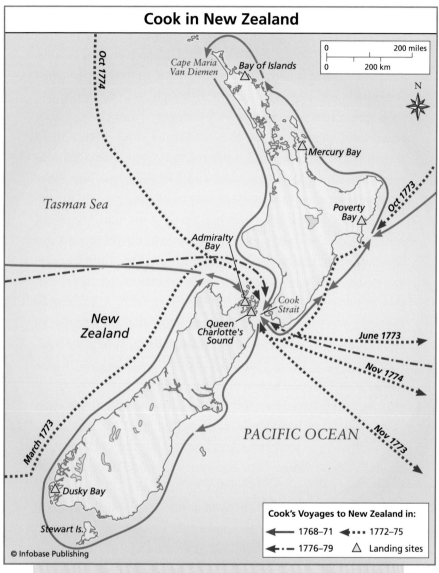

Cook in New Zealand

Oct 1774

Cape Maria
Van Diemen   *Bay of Islands*

0   200 miles

0   200 km

N

Mercury Bay

Tasman Sea

Poverty
Bay

Oct 1773

Admiralty
Bay

*New
Zealand*

Cook
Strait

Queen
Charlotte's
Sound

June 1773

Nov 1774

March 1773

PACIFIC OCEAN

Nov 1773

Dusky Bay

Stewart Is.

© Infobase Publishing

Cook's Voyages to New Zealand in:

1768–71   1772–75

1776–79   △ Landing sites

Dutch explorer Abel Tasman was the first European known to reach
New Zealand in 1642. Cook first visited the islands more than 100
years after Tasman, between 1769–1770, and renamed them *New
Zealand* from the Dutch *Nieuw Zeeland*. During this voyage, Cook
discovered that New Zealand was not attached to a larger landmass
to the south, but instead consisted of two main islands (and numerous smaller islands).

a high hill from which he saw "the Eastern Sea, and a strait or passage from it into the Western Sea."

Banks and some of Cook's officers, however, had doubts. They still thought North Island might be part of a peninsula attached to a southern continent. Although, as Cook wrote, "no such supposition ever entered my thoughts," on February 2, he sailed the *Endeavour* through what is now Cook's Strait, then turned north until he once more reached Cape Turnagain. He then called his officers together and had them tell him "they were now satisfied that this land was an island."

Even so, some still believed that a continent lay to the south of Cook's Strait. The next two months would prove them wrong. As the *Endeavour* struggled toward the south in ever-worsening weather, more people became convinced, like Cook, that this was not a continent but another island. According to Hough's *Captain James Cook*, Banks wrote that the number of "we Continents" was now down to himself and "one poor midshipman." On March 9, South Cape was rounded and Banks had to admit that he was wrong.

Eighteen days later, the *Endeavour* was back at the strait between the two islands. Cook docked at what he later called Admiralty Cove, and three days later he left the northwest tip of South Island, called Cape Farewell. He would have preferred to head for England the same way he had come—around Cape Horn—but he would have arrived at the cape after the onset of winter and the waters were too rough. Instead, he decided to head west, south of Australia and on to the Cape of Good Hope in Africa.

Australia

On April 19, 1770, Lieutenant Hicks spotted land—what is now called Point Hicks—from a vantage point high on the foremast. Cook continued, intending to sail south of Van Diemen's Land, later to be named Tasmania after Abel Tasman. Cook was puzzled to find open water south of Point Hicks, however, since he had not known that Tasmania is an island.

He could have turned west, discovering the Bass Strait between Tasmania and Australia and continuing his planned course, but the urge to explore was too great. Tasman had charted Australia from its westernmost point to the northernmost tip, but no one had seen the east coast. Cook resolved to be the first.

He turned north, seeking a place to take on food and water, but it was a week before he could find a suitable location. Finally, the *Endeavour* dropped its anchor in what Cook eventually named Botany Bay because of the marvelous variety of plants on shore.

It was here that Cook and his men got their first close look at the Aborigines, whom they had seen only from a great distance while sailing up the coast. Cook's journal describes them as "of a very dark brown colour" with hair "black and lank like ours." They seemed very uninterested in their visitors, Banks wrote, and, as quoted by Hough, they "expressed neither surprise nor concern," but seemed "totally unmoved at us."

The next day, Cook took a small boat close to the shore. Tupaia tried to communicate with the Aborigines, but they replied in a language he could not understand. When Cook and his party came on shore, the Aborigines fled. They later returned, armed with what the Europeans took to be short swords but which were actually boomerangs. They retreated only after the Europeans fired muskets over their heads.

Without trading with the Aborigines, the *Endeavour* resumed its voyage on May 6, passing Port Jackson harbor, where the city of Sydney would one day stand. The ship worked its way north along the coast, pausing periodically to allow Banks and the scientists to go ashore to gather plants and to try—unsuccessfully—to establish communications with the Aborigines.

The Great Barrier Reef

The *Endeavour* approached the Tropic of Capricorn (one of the five major circles of latitude that mark maps of the Earth) on May 24. Cook noticed small waves, or breakers, extending out to the northeast. Over the next few days, he encountered numerous small islands and increasingly shoal, or shallow, water. He could not know it, but the *Endeavour* had entered the treacherous passage between the mainland and the Great Barrier Reef.

For two weeks, Cook worked the ship through what he would later call in his journal an "insane labyrinth." From June 3 on, a man was stationed "in the chains," or hanging over the bow, casting a line weighted with lead to judge depth. On June 11, at about 11:00 P.M., the water grew abruptly shallower and, as Cook wrote, "before the man could heave another cast, the ship struck and stuck fast."

Banks, quoted in Nicholas Thomas's *Cook*, wrote that the ship was "beating very violently against the rocks" and that "we were upon sunken coral rocks, the most dreadful of all others on account of their sharp points and grinding quality, which cut through a ship's bottom almost immediately." The *Endeavour* was in grave danger. The ship had struck at high tide, so there was no question of being lifted off. The movement of the ship by breakers brought about a grinding on the hull that eventually would have destroyed it. If the ship sank, the nearest land was 20 miles away, and there were not enough boats to carry everyone to safety.

Cook first attempted to kedge the ship—or move it along—by using the cable of one of the ship's secondary anchors. The anchor was put in a boat, rowed a distance from the ship, and dropped. The *Endeavour*'s crew then heaved on the capstan (the cylinder around which the cable is wound), trying to pull the ship off the reef. It would not budge. Cook's next move was to lighten the ship. Tons of firewood, stone and iron ballast from the hold, and casks of water were discarded.

Even the guns and anchors went overboard, although they were marked with buoys for later recovery.

The men labored furiously at the three pumps, working in 15-minute shifts. Even so, the amount of water coming in through the hole in the hull increased. As quoted by Hough in *Captain James Cook*, Banks wrote that the men "worked with surprising cheerfulness," and Cook would even say in his journal, "I must say that no men ever behaved better."

Cook knew that the next high tide would come at about 10:00 P.M. on June 12, and with it came the best chance of floating the ship off the reef. Still, it would be a gamble. Once free, the ship might take on so much water that it would sink.

He decided to take the risk, and it paid off. When the time came, the men at the capstan strained against the anchor cable, and the *Endeavour* floated free. Now, at least, the leak could be reduced. Midshipman Monkhouse once had witnessed someone stop a leak by a method called fothering, and now he put his experience to good use. A spare sail was covered with tar and wool, and then passed under the ship until it covered and was pressed into the hole. With this patch in place, only one pump was necessary during the five days it took to get the ship to a safe anchorage where it could be beached and repaired.

The ship would remain by present-day Endeavour River for almost two months—first to repair the ship and then to wait for a favorable wind. When the *Endeavour* was beached and careened, or tipped over on one side, Cook could see how lucky he had been. A large piece of coral had broken off from the reef and was lodged in the hole through the hull. Had that not happened, the ship probably would have sunk once it was off the reef.

Underway Again

Finally, on August 13, the *Endeavour*, only partially repaired, was able to cautiously make its way northward. A week later, it had cleared the Great Barrier Reef. As he passed the northernmost point of Australia, which he named Cape York, he went

After making several discoveries on Botany Bay, Cook and his crew continued to sail north along the Australian coast. On June 11, 1770, disaster struck when the *Endeavor* ran aground on the Great Barrier Reef and sustained significant damage. The immovable ship was finally able to re-float during an incoming tide, after the crew had considerably lightened its load.

ashore and, in the words of his journal, "once more hoisted English colours [the flag] and in the name of His Majesty King George the Third took possession of the whole eastern coast . . . by the name of New South Wales."

The *Endeavour*'s route now lay along the southern coast of New Guinea and past the island of Timor to the city of Batavia—now Jakarta—on the east end of the island of Java. A few days after reaching the city on October 11, Cook wrote to the Admiralty. He sent the letter to London, along with his maps and journals, by way of a Dutch ship. In it he boasted, as quoted by Beaglehole, that "I have not lost one man by sickness during the whole voyage." Sadly, that would soon no longer be true.

There had been deaths—some from accidents, one suicide, one from epilepsy, and one from tuberculosis—but none from such common maladies as ship fever or scurvy. Batavia, however, had been laid out by the Dutch colonists as if it were in Holland, complete with canals. In tropical Java, however, such canals had become filthy breeding grounds for malaria and other diseases, and Batavia was one of the least healthy cities on Earth.

Sickness—mostly dysentery—swept through the crew to the point where only 20 men were healthy enough to work. Doctor William Monkhouse died on November 5 and was followed shortly after by his assistant William Perry and four more crewmen. The two Tahitians, Tupaia and Tiata, also died. Banks and Solander were seriously ill, but they survived after moving to a house high up on a hill and dosing themselves with quinine.

On December 26, 1770, repairs were completed and supplies had been brought aboard by the remaining crew. The *Endeavour*, which Cook now called in his journal "my hospital ship," set sail, with many in the crew still very ill. A marine corporal, John Truslove, died on January 24 to be followed by Spöring, Parkinson, and the astronomer, Charles Green. Four more crewmen died a week later, and the first week in February claimed six more, including Jonathan Monkhouse.

By the time the ship reached Cape Town, South Africa, on March 14, 1771, 34 men had died and another 30 were seriously ill. Five more, including Lieutenant Hicks and Master Robert Molyneaux, died either in the hospital on shore or during the final part of the journey back to England, which began on April 16. In all, 39 members of the crew died after the stay in Batavia.

It was, therefore, something of a somber homecoming when the *Endeavour* dropped anchor off the English coast at the port of Deal on July 13, 1771, after a voyage of 2 years and 11 months. In his earlier letter to the Admiralty, Cook had written, as quoted in Alistair Maclean's *Captain Cook*, "The discoveries made in this voyage are not great." He could not have been more wrong. The voyage of the *Endeavour* had opened the South Pacific to Great Britain and would eventually lead to the inclusion of Australia and New Zealand in the British Empire. What Cook, in his modesty, could not have imagined was that even greater discoveries lay ahead.

England, 1771–1772

COOK'S MODEST ASSESSMENT OF HIS FIRST VOYAGE WAS SHARED by practically no one else. The Admiralty thoroughly approved and said so. The public thought so, too, but it was Banks who sought—and received—most of the credit. Everyone was eager for a second voyage, this one to seek the elusive southern continent, but it would take a year of preparation—and dealing with Banks's ego—before it would be ready.

Cook's first stop in London was the Admiralty, where he gave a brief report to Secretary Philip Stevens, and from there to his home on Assembly Row. His sons James and Nathaniel were now eight and six years old, but his daughter, Elizabeth, had died three months earlier and his son Joseph, who had been born shortly after the *Endeavour* sailed, had only lived three months.

There was plenty to keep him busy. He wrote reports to the Admiralty and dozens of letters. Some probably gave him pleasure—such as recommendations for promotions—while

Naval exploration increased immensely during the eighteenth century, as each newly discovered land became a symbol of power for competing nations. British explorers like Cook were supported in their efforts by the Admiralty, the former authority in the United Kingdom that commanded the Royal Navy. Above is a depiction of the Admiralty complex.

others, like those to the relatives of his men who had died, were more difficult.

There were two letters he was happy to receive in August. According to Hough's *Captain James Cook*, the first, from Secretary Stevens said that "the Board extremely well approve of the whole of his proceedings." The second was from Banks, informing him that he had learned from his friend Lord Sandwich that Cook had been promoted from lieutenant to commander.

Banks, meanwhile, was the toast of London. He visited regularly with King George, although he did bring Cook along on one occasion. At Oxford University, where he received an honorary doctorate, writes Hough, he was called "the immortal Banks." And Beaglehole's *The Life of Captain James Cook* adds that the noted Swedish botanist Carl Linnaeus proposed that New South Wales be renamed Banksia. Some of the newspaper accounts of the voyage praised Banks while barely mentioning Cook or ignoring him altogether.

One report toward the end of August, as quoted by Hough's *Captain James Cook*, even reported that "Mr. Banks is to have two ships from government to pursue his discoveries ... and will sail upon his second voyage next March." Cook was, at least, aware of this. He wrote to John Walker, his old employer in Whitby, that he expected to be named to lead this second voyage.

The Suggested Route

Cook already had been thinking about such an expedition and had written suggestions to the Admiralty. He proposed that it sail first to Cape Town and then to New Zealand. From there, after taking on food and water, it would explore the far southern latitudes of the Pacific. If no continent were found, the voyage would continue to Tahiti, spend the winter there, then round Cape Horn to search the southern latitudes of the Atlantic.

Cook also recommended that a ship larger than the *Endeavour* be used and, possibly remembering the anxious hours stuck on the reef, that a second ship be added. The navy agreed and in early November bought the *Marquis of Granby* and the *Marquis of Rockingham*, both having been built in Whitby along the same lines as the *Endeavour*. The ships were renamed the *Drake* and the *Raleigh* after two famous English explorers, but someone remembered that Spain (their longtime rival), which still maintained a claim to the Pacific, might take offense. The names were changed to more neutral ones, this time to the *Resolution* and the *Adventure*.

Cook had hoped that the expedition would sail in March 1772, but he didn't reckon on Banks. Newspapers had been referring to "Mr. Banks's voyage" for so long that the botanist had come to believe that he would be in virtual command with Cook as a sort of chauffeur. He began assembling his scientific team, choosing from among hundreds of applicants from all over Europe, and finally settled on 15 people, including not only scientists but personal servants and, for entertainment, two horn players.

Banks's Demands

The real trouble began when Banks first inspected the *Resolution*, which was to be his and Cook's ship. The accommodations, he protested, were far too small for him and his attendants. He demanded that the waist, or middle, of the ship be raised to include an extra deck. Furthermore, he wanted a small cabin built on the poop, or rear, deck for Cook so that he could have the main cabin all to himself.

Palliser, now treasurer of the navy, refused the demands, but Banks went over his head, appealing to Lord Sandwich, who agreed. It appeared to Cook that the *Resolution* would be dangerously top-heavy, yet he could do nothing but watch with alarm as work continued through the proposed March sailing date and well into April. The speed of the renovation was not helped by Banks bringing his admirers on board. Beaglehole quotes Cook writing, in a rare ironic moment, about "Ladies as well as Gentlemen . . . who came on board for no other purpose but to see the ship in which Mr. Banks was to sail round the world."

COOK'S OPINION OF JOSEPH BANKS

Originally, Joseph Banks, who led the scientific portion of Cook's first voyage, was to have the same responsibility on the second. When the modifications he had made to the *Resolution* were dismantled, however, he elected to charter his own ship and undertake an exploration of Iceland instead. In his journal, Cook reflected on the incident:

> To many it will no doubt appear strange that Mr. Banks should attempt to overrule the opinions of the two great boards who have the sole management of the whole navy of Great Britain and likewise the opinions of the principal sea officers concerned in the expedition; for a gentleman of Mr. Banks's fortune and abilities to engage in these kinds of voyages is as uncommon as it is meritorious and the great additions he made last voyage to the systems of botany and natural history gained him great reputation which was increased by his embarking in this [voyage]. This, together with a desire in everyone to make things as convenient to him as possible, made him to be consulted on every occasion and his influence was so great that his opinion was generally followed, was it ever so inconsistent, in preference to those who from their long experience in sea affairs might be supposed better judges, till at length the sloop [*Resolution*] was rendered unfit for any service whatever.

The *Resolution*, as altered, would not sail very far at all. On May 14, John Palliser Cooper, who was to be Cook's first lieutenant, was ordered to take the ship from its dock just west of London down the Thames River and to the port of Deal on the southeastern coast. The pilot, or harbor officer charged with guiding the ship down the river, gave up after a few miles, fearful of capsizing. Cooper, as quoted by Beaglehole, told Cook that the *Resolution* was "an exceeding dangerous and unsafe ship." Charles Clerke, the second lieutenant, wrote to Banks, as quoted by Nicholas Thomas in *Cook: The Extraordinary Voyages of Captain James Cook*, "By God, I'll go to sea in a grog-tub [a tub in which water and rum were mixed] if required . . . but I think her the most unsafe ship I ever saw or heard of."

The *Resolution* was promptly returned to the shipyard, where all the alterations were undone. When Banks saw what had happened, wrote Midshipman John Elliot as quoted by Hough, he "swore and stamped upon the wharf like a madman; and instantly ordered his servants, and all his things out of the ship."

Banks protested to Lord Sandwich in a letter almost 2,000 words long, in which he threatened to make his objections public. The First Lord's reply was quick, brief, and to the point. He wrote back that the Admiralty would go public, too, for it is "a heavy charge . . . to send a number of men to sea in an unhealthy ship." Banks realized he had lost, but rather than accept what had been done, he chartered his own ship and set out for an exploration of Iceland.

Banks's place as chief scientist was taken by the brilliant but cantankerous Johann Förster, who brought along as a draftsman his son George. William Wales and William Bayly were the astronomers, and William Hodges was the artist.

The Question of Longitude

Astronomers were required on this voyage because of another aspect of Cook's mission. Calculating longitude was a difficult and inexact task that depended on lunar observations. What was needed was a clock that would show Greenwich Mean, or London, Time. By comparing that time with local time, a ship's position east or west of London could be calculated easily.

During Cook's time, sailors were unable to calculate longitude at sea, or how far apart two places on Earth are from east or west. The motions of a ship and changes in humidity and temperature prevented clocks from keeping accurate time at sea. Cook's second voyage proved that longitude finally could be measured from a watch. Pictured is a copy of one of John Harrison's chronometers, made by Larcum and Kendall, with testimony by Cook praising its accuracy.

So far, however, no one had been able to design a clock that would keep time aboard a moving ship and in extreme temperatures, with the required degree of accuracy. The most promising was one by John Harrison, a Yorkshire carpenter. His first effort had weighed 75 pounds, but his latest version weighed only three pounds and had a diameter of five inches. A London watchmaker made an exact replica, which was taken on board the *Resolution* to be tested against four other timepieces made by an inventor named John Arnold.

In addition to the scientists, there were 112 officers and men on the *Resolution* and 81 on the smaller *Adventure*. In addition to Cooper and Clerke, Cook's other lieutenant was Richard Pickersgill, who had been promoted from warrant officer. Joseph Gilbert was the master, and Edgcumbe again commanded the marines. Tobias Furneaux was the lieutenant commanding the *Adventure*, assisted by lieutenants Joseph Shank and Arthur Kempe. Notable among the midshipmen were James "Jem" Burney, brother of novelist Fanny Burney and a future admiral, and George Vancouver, the future explorer for whom the capital of Canadian British Columbia is named.

By June, all the provisions were on board including other experiments—carrot marmalade thought to fight scurvy, dehydrated beer, and a machine for making salt water fresh. On June 21, Cook said good-bye to his again-pregnant wife and his children. The next day, the *Resolution* weighed anchor and sailed for Plymouth, joining the *Adventure* there on July 3. Ten days later, the two ships set out, Pickersgill writing in his journal, as quoted by Beaglehole, "Farewell Old England." It would be many months and there would be many adventures before anyone on board saw Old England again.

The Second Voyage, 1772–1775

JAMES COOK'S SECOND VOYAGE STANDS AS ONE OF THE MOST remarkable in the annals of exploration, covering almost 70,000 miles in 36 months. He became the first man to penetrate the Antarctic Circle, doing so not once, but three times in search of a continent he suspected did not exist. In between these plunges southward, he and his men resumed their exploration of the Pacific, making new discoveries and expanding on previous ones.

Once at sea, Cook quickly began applying the same regimen of cleanliness and diet as he had on the first voyage. New crewmen grumbled at the frequency with which they had to wash their clothes, their quarters, and themselves. They turned up their noses at sauerkraut, but they ate it under threat of the lash. As a result, when the ships reached the tip of Africa on November 30, not a man on the *Resolution* was ill, whereas on the *Adventure*, two midshipmen had died and the first lieutenant was so ill he had to be sent home.

Cook spent three weeks in Cape Town, South Africa. While waiting on fresh supplies, he took time to write to John Walker in Whitby, as quoted by Thomas, that "When I think of the inhospitable parts I am going to, I think the voyage dangerous; I, however, enter upon it with great cheerfulness."

When the expedition sailed in November, its first objective was to seek "Cape Circumcision," so named in 1739 by the French explorer Bouvet. Bouvet placed it about 1,600 miles south of Cape Town and thought it part of a southern continent. A second goal was to investigate something Cook had heard in Cape Town—that the French explorer Kerguelen-Trémarec had found what he thought might be part of a southern continent in the direction Cook would soon be heading.

As the *Resolution* and *Adventure* headed south, the weather quickly turned cold. Nearly all the livestock brought on board at Cape Town died. Icebergs began to appear, and so did the crew's fearnought jackets. Cook wrote in his journal that although the icebergs might be "pleasing to the eye . . . the mind is filled with horror" at the danger they posed to ships.

By the time they reached the latitude indicated by Bouvet, a gale had pushed them more than 300 miles too far east. Cook decided he could not take the time to double back, and he abandoned the search. "Cape Circumcision" eventually would turn out to be not a cape, but Bouvet Island.

Crossing the Circle

Cook then pressed farther south, believing that the southern continent—if it existed at all, which he doubted—would be much farther in that direction. He picked his way through the ice fields, and on January 17 he crossed the Antarctic Circle at latitude 66 degrees, 33 minutes south of the equator. Cook allowed himself a small boast in his journal that they were "undoubtedly the first and only ship that ever crossed that line." He

During the second voyage, Cook's flagship, the *Resolution*, and the smaller ship, the *Adventure*, commanded by Tobias Furneaux, sailed some 10,600 miles through uncharted waters, heavy storms, and dangerous seas filled with enormous icebergs.

could not have known that he was, at that point, only about 100 miles from Antarctica.

The ice was too thick, however, for him to go farther south, and he turned northeast, spending a week searching the area where Kerguelen-Trémarec had reported a discovery. He found nothing, prompting Lieutenant Clerke to write, as quoted by Hough, that "our friends the French were only amusing the good folks at the Cape with a little of the marvelous." As it turned out, accidentally or not, Cook had been given an incorrect position. What he sought lay many miles to the east and was not part of a continent, but instead were the Kerguelen Islands.

The ships continued eastward, north of the Antarctic Circle but still far south of any known exploration. The weather worsened, gales alternating with thick fog. On February 8, after one particularly dense fog cleared, the *Resolution* found, wrote Clerke as quoted by Hough, that "to our great mortification we found [the *Adventure*] was not within our horizons." When the *Adventure* could not be found after three days of searching, Cook assumed that Furneaux had followed the plan that, if such a separation occurred, they would rendezvous at Queen Charlotte Sound in New Zealand. It is the easternmost of the main sounds in South Island.

Cook, however, was not ready to head north. There was still time, before the Antarctic winter set in, for exploring, so he, writing in his journal, "resolved to get as far to the south as I could," passing about 300 miles north of Antarctica. Foul weather, longer nights, and the constant threat from icebergs, however, kept him from his goal of crossing the Antarctic Circle once more. His men were exhausted, their clothes in tatters. On March 17, he wrote that anyone reading his journal would consider it "natural for me to wish to enjoy some repose in a harbour where I can procure some refreshments for my people." Accordingly, he changed course for New Zealand.

Dusky Bay

Cook's target, however, was not Queen Charlotte Sound but Dusky Bay, which he had noted as a promising harbor on his first voyage. It was much closer, located at the southwest tip of South Island, and it is an indication of the condition of the crew that he headed there first, reaching it on March 23 (see page 7).

After the rigors of the Antarctic, Dusky Bay must have seemed like paradise. Wood and fresh water were abundant and close at hand. The bay was full of fish and the woods were full of ducks. Seals were hunted both for their blubber to be used as fuel and for their flesh, which was favorably compared to roast beef. "We expected to enjoy with ease what in our situation might be called the luxuries of life," Cook wrote.

The *Resolution* remained at Dusky Bay until May 11 when, stores full and crew fit and rested, it sailed north for Queen Charlotte Sound. While almost everyone was sorry to leave such an idyllic spot, the cantankerous Johann Förster was typically sour, writing, as quoted by Beaglehole, how glad he was to be leaving "this dirty, and, on that account, disagreeable place."

A week later, the ship reached Ship Cove in Queen Charlotte Sound. Cook was relieved to see the *Adventure* waiting there, having arrived six weeks earlier. He was disappointed, however, to learn that Furneaux's crew, as he wrote, had been "much afflicted with the scurvy."

Furneaux had set up tents on shore and had moved most of his supplies from the ship, intending—Cook thought—to spend the winter in ease. Furneaux, however, assumed they would be ashore without Cook, who had no intention of remaining idle for months. Instead, he was told that the ships would sail as soon as they could be made ready and that the plan was to sail east for almost 2,000 miles looking for any sign of a southern continent, to turn north, and then to make a sweep westward to Tahiti and beyond, remaining in that vicinity before returning to New Zealand for another season in the Antarctic.

It would be another three weeks before the ships were ready. During this time, the crew engaged in trade with the Maoris, who were much less warlike than those encountered on the first voyage. Cook noted that, as with the Tahitians, iron objects were prized and that a man might prostitute his wife or daughter in order to get one. This led him to write, rather philosophically, that "such are the consequences of a commerce with Europeans, we ... introduce among them wants and perhaps diseases which they never before knew and which serve only to disturb that happy tranquility they and their forefathers enjoyed. If anyone denies the truth of this assertion let him tell me what the natives of the whole extent of America have gained by the commerce they have had with Europeans."

Toward Tahiti

The ships sailed from New Zealand on June 7 and headed east for almost seven weeks, finding nothing. In late July, Cook turned north, hoping to find Pitcairn Island, discovered seven years earlier by Philip Carteret. Shortly afterward, however, scurvy broke out on the *Adventure*. Cook was frustrated and angry that Furneaux obviously had not followed Cook's strict instructions about diet. Cook understood that sailors tended to resist any innovations in diet, but he wrote that sometimes "the examples and authority of a commander" are required.

The ships turned west and two weeks later were at Tahiti. Some of the crewmen were so ill that Cook, instead of sailing around the island to the familiar Matavai Bay, anchored at the first opportunity in Vaitepiha Bay.

When eventually they did reach their old anchorage, Cook and his men received a tumultuous welcome. Cook, hoping to get the visit off to a good start, invited a chief and his party on board the *Resolution*. The visitors were soon openly pilfering as before, even handing items through the railing to those in the canoes alongside. Finally, Cook, as he wrote, felt compelled to "turn them all out of the ship."

Huahine

Cook had hoped to replenish his food supply, including fresh meat, but he found that recent tribal warfare had limited hog breeding. As a result, he remained in Tahiti only two weeks, and on September 1 he set out for other islands with whose inhabitants he could trade. Neighboring Huahine was just the spot.

During his travels, Cook and his crew often took along native Pacific Islanders to serve as interpreters. One of those that traveled with Cook was Omai, a young Ra'iatean man who joined the *Adventure* during the second expedition. Omai was the first Pacific Islander to visit Europe when the *Adventure* returned to London in October 1774.

The chief remembered Cook and greeted him like an old friend, and there was no lack of food for which to trade. Clerke wrote, as quoted by Hough, about "great plenty of hogs coming from all quarters" and the Huahinians providing "most plentifully in pork, yams, plantains, etc."

Besides food, Cook picked up two passengers. A young man named Omai convinced Furneaux to take him on board the *Adventure*, and another young man named Hitihiti—but whom the crew nicknamed Odiddy—came aboard the *Resolution* as an interpreter, much as Tupaia had done on the first voyage.

Although his plan called for a return to New Zealand, Cook never could resist the urge to explore just a little farther. So, instead of sailing east, the *Resolution* and the *Adventure* went west to find the island group that had been reported in the previous century by Tasman. On October 1, Cook sighted one of the three main islands, the one Tasman had named Middleburg.

The people there, however, did not seem much interested in trade, so Cook moved to the next island—Tasman's Amsterdam—where he had no trouble finding enough supplies. Indeed, wrote William Wales, as quoted by Hough, "the island seems to be in the highest state of cultivation, there being scarce a foot of land which is not enclosed and planted." Here, too, the crew received a warm welcome, so much so that Cook named the group the Friendly Islands, now known by their original name, Tonga.

Back to New Zealand

It was now time to sail, however, and two weeks later the ships reached New Zealand's North Island. As they headed toward Queen Charlotte's Sound, Cook wrote, a storm "came on in such fury as to oblige us to take in all our sails . . . and to lay-to under our bare poles." The ships had to stand well out to sea to avoid being blown ashore, and they eventually lost sight of each other. When he was able, after two weeks of such weather, Cook took the *Resolution* into Ship Cove. He hoped to find the *Adventure* awaiting him, but it was nowhere to be seen.

Two weeks went by with no sign of the other ship. Cook feared the *Adventure* had gone down or perhaps that its crew had been forced ashore and had been attacked by the Maoris—and he and his men knew what happened to Maori victims. They had heard stories about cannibalism on the first voyage, but now they had proof after Lieutenant Pickersgill had bought a recently severed head as a curiosity and had brought it on the ship. A visiting Maori had asked if he could have it and, when questioned why, had answered that he wanted to eat it and promptly did so in front of Cook and the horrified Europeans.

Cook took a tolerant view of Maori cannibalism, which was limited to eating enemies killed in battle. He wrote that the practice "has undoubtedly been handed down to them from the earliest times and we know that it is not an easy matter to break a nation of its ancient customs let them be ever so inhuman and savage." The custom would disappear, he was confident, when New Zealand became more civilized.

The men of the *Adventure* would, indeed, suffer at the hands of the Maoris. When the storm had subsided, Furneaux was able to find a harbor in Tolago Bay on North Island and was only able to reach Ship Cove in early December. By that time, however, Cook was gone. He had departed on November 25, leaving a note for Furneaux that gave him a general idea of where he would be going, but which also allowed him to act on his own. The *Adventure* had taken such a pounding in the storm that Furneaux, who seemingly did not share Cook's passion for exploring, decided to return to England.

On December 17, however, Midshipman John Rowe and nine men took a ship's boat and went ashore at Grass Cove to gather wild vegetables. They failed to return, and the next morning Lieutenant Burney took another boat ashore with a party of heavily armed marines to search for them. After chasing a band of Maoris from a beach, they found, Burney wrote, as quoted by Beaglehole, "such a shocking scene of carnage and barbarity as can never be mentioned or thought of but with horror." The scene included clothes and shoes belonging

WHAT THE MEN THOUGHT OF COOK

Despite being at times a hard disciplinarian, James Cook held the utmost respect and affection from the members of his crew. One of his sailors, Heinrich Zimmerman, gave this description, found on the Captain Cook Society Web site:

> Captain Cook was a tall, handsome, strong, but somewhat spare man. His hair was dark brown, his expression somewhat stern, and his shoulders bent.... He was inexorable regarding the ship's regulations and the punishments connected with them so much so, indeed, that if, when we were amongst the natives, anything was stolen from us by them the man on watch at the time was severely punished for his neglect.... No officer ever presumed to contradict him. When at table with his officers he frequently sat without saying a word. He was, in fact, very reserved....
>
> He never mentioned religion, and would have no priests on his ships; and, although he seldom celebrated the Sabbath, he was a just and upright man in all his dealings. He never swore, not even when in a rage. He was scrupulously clean, and the example which he set in this direction had to be followed by every man on board. It was a regulation that every member of the crew should put on clean clothes every Sunday.

to Rowe's men, a hand they identified as a crewmate's from a tattoo, and—worst of all—heads and body parts.

Burney's men took some revenge by destroying all the canoes they found on the beach. When they returned to the *Adventure* and reported what they had seen, the crew wanted to destroy every canoe in Ship Cove and burn all the villages in the area. Furneaux, however, could see no point in retaliating against the entire population, and the *Adventure* left New Zealand that afternoon.

Meanwhile, the crew of the *Resolution*, Cook wrote, were not overly disturbed at having no companion ship, but instead "cheerfully proceeded ... wherever I thought proper to lead them." That "wherever" would turn out to be the Antarctic. By December 12, the crew had spotted the first iceberg and the temperature had fallen to 32°F (0°C). Nine days later Clerke wrote, as quoted by Hough, that so much sleet froze to the rigging that it was "with difficulty we render the ropes through the blocks."

The Antarctic

On December 27, a crewman named Jack Marra wrote, as quoted by Hough, that "icicles frequently hung to the noses of the men more than an inch long" and that they were "cased in frozen snow, as if clad in armour." Two weeks later, Cook altered his course, turning to the northeast. The crew cheered up, thinking they might be homeward bound, but just two days later the *Resolution* was once more headed south.

On January 26, the ship crossed the Antarctic Circle for the third time, and three days later it penetrated to 71°10'S (latitude 71 degrees, 10 minutes south), and longitude (as given by Kendall's watch) 106°54'W (106 degrees, 54 minutes west). That point remains the farthest ever reached by ship in that part of the Antarctic. According to a later account by Vancouver, as quoted by Richard Hough's *Captain James Cook*, Cook was determined to be the man who ventured nearer to the South Pole than any other had done. He went to the very tip of the bowsprit—the mast projecting from the front of the ship—waved his hat in the frigid air, and shouted, "Ne plus ultra," Latin for "No more beyond."

Before the *Resolution* lay an immense field of ice that stretched from one end of the horizon to the other. The ice, Cook wrote, was so packed together that "nothing could enter it." Even to try, he wrote, would be "a very dangerous enterprise." He had come as far as possible and was resolved to head back north. "I who hope ambition leads me not only further than any other man has been, but as far as I think it is possible for man to go, was not sorry at meeting with this interruption."

Cook was more convinced than ever that a southern continent, if it did exist, was beyond humanity's reach. "The greatest part of this Southern Continent," he wrote, "must lie within the Polar Circle, where the sea is so pestered with ice that the land is thereby inaccessible.... I can be bold enough to say, that no man will ever venture farther than I have done, and that the lands which lie to the south will never be explored."

Extended Voyage

His mission had been accomplished, but Cook's zest for adventure would not let him head for home. He had a sound ship and a healthy crew, and there was still much to be explored in the Pacific. He called his men together and proposed that the voyage be extended for as much as a year—that the *Resolution* try to find Easter Island, which was first spotted by Dutchman Jacob Roggeveen more than 50 years earlier, and then sweep back west across the Pacific on a new route that would extend almost to Australia before visiting New Zealand once more and then heading for Cape Town and England. The officers, Cook wrote, "heartily concurred" with the plan, and the crewmen "rejoiced at the prospect of [the voyage] being prolonged."

As the *Resolution* made her way due north, Cook became ill. Never one to dwell on himself, he wrote in his journal only about "the bilious colic, which was so violent as to confine me to my bed." It was evidently much more serious. Marra noted, as quoted by Hough, that "the Captain was taken ill, to the grief of all the ship's company." This was a testament to the high regard the crew had for Cook, which was perhaps one reason why they had so readily agreed to extend the voyage.

George Förster, the draftsman, wrote, as quoted by Beagle-hole, that Cook first "was pale and lean, entirely lost his appetite, and laboured under a perpetual costiveness [constipation]." He appeared, for a time, to have recovered somewhat, but then he suffered a relapse. Only a week's worth of skillful treatment by the ship's doctor, James Patten, with hot baths and hot plasters applied to his torso, George Förster wrote, "relaxed his body and intestines."

Meanwhile, as the ship headed north, the Antarctic cold yielded to warm, tropical breezes. Indeed, it grew so uncomfortably hot that Wales wrote, as quoted by Beaglehole, "it's scarcely three weeks ago we were miserable on account of the cold; we are now wretched with the heat." In addition to the heat, the crew suffered from a lack of fresh food, having eaten nothing but salt beef, pork, and biscuits for 14 weeks.

Easter Island

Easter Island was sighted on March 11. Cook wrote that he could see through his telescope "those monuments or idols" mentioned by Roggeveen. The *Resolution* dropped anchor the next day, and much-needed food was acquired in exchange for nails. The islanders, Cook noted, were of the same Polynesian stock as the Tahitians, as evidenced by "the affinity of the language, colour and some of their customs." Cook marveled that "the same nation [people] should have spread themselves

In 1774, about 50 years after the first recorded contact, Cook and his crew landed at Easter Island with a Tahitian interpreter. The island that had once been lined at its shore with stone statues was now described as neglected. Some of the statues had fallen down and his botanist described it as a "poor land."

all over . . . this vast ocean from New Zealand to this island," almost a fourth of the way around the world.

He and the crew also marveled at the great stone statues, which were much like other Polynesian figures they had seen, only on a gigantic scale. Wales, as quoted by Thomas, thought that they had been "erected to the memory of some of their ancient chiefs," which turned out to be correct. Cook saw no great mystery as to how the statues had been placed upright, writing that the top end was probably raised bit by bit, with stones or logs placed underneath each time, until the entire figure could be slid into a hole.

The *Resolution* had acquired food, but not enough, and there had been no sufficient supply of fresh water. So, after less than a week at Easter Island, Cook sailed on toward Tahiti. On the way, Cook suffered another attack similar to the one before, but Patten again pulled him through. He seems to have been fully recovered when the Marquesas Islands were sighted on April 6. There was plenty of fresh water on the islands, as well as fruits and vegetables, but livestock was scarce.

By April 21, the *Resolution* was back in Tahiti, and the crew received the customary warm welcome. The island's economy had recovered from the tribal warfare of the previous year, and livestock was plentiful. Huahine and Raiatea were the next ports of call, with Odiddy bidding a tearful farewell at the latter, but instead of heading for New Zealand, Cook pressed on to Tonga, reaching the islands on June 27.

Tonga

The people of Tonga were as friendly as before, but, as Clerke wrote, quoted by Hough, "very industrious in the pilfering scheme." Muskets were a favorite target, and Cook adopted a practice of seizing a number of canoes from a chief and threatening to burn them if the stolen goods were not returned. It usually worked.

The Tongans were fascinated by firearms, and Cook obliged them by having his marines conduct an exhibition of marksmanship. He did not want the islanders to become too familiar with muskets, however, fearing they might learn that "firearms were not such terrible things as they had imagined," and that they, at almost any time they wished, could overwhelm the Europeans with superior numbers.

After a few weeks in Tonga, Cook took a roundabout route to New Zealand, sailing northwest into the islands seen by Spain's Pedro Quirós in 1606. Cook named them the New Hebrides, and found their people to be far different from those of most places he had visited. Shorter, darker, and speaking another language, these were Melanesians rather than Polynesians. They were much more hostile, as well, and it was only with difficulty that any trade took place. Cook could not blame them, though, reflecting on how Europeans had come uninvited to these islands, forcing themselves on the inhabitants: "In what other light can they than at first look upon us but as invaders," he wrote.

Proceeding south, Cook found a warmer welcome at the large island he named New Caledonia. The next stop was an uninhabited island on which grew giant pine trees. Cook claimed the island for England and named it Norfolk, and the trees became known as Norfolk pines.

It was only a short distance to New Zealand, and the *Resolution* was in Ship Cove by the morning of October 18. There were no Maoris to greet them, though it was only six days later that a canoe was spotted, which quickly turned around when its occupants saw the ship. At length, contact was made and trade began, but Cook and his men began to hear strange stories. A group of strange men had come ashore, the Maoris said, and they were killed and eaten. But, the Maoris were quick to say that they had not done this and it had happened elsewhere. This made Cook more concerned than ever about Furneaux and his men.

The *Resolution* was in need of repair, forcing Cook to spend almost a month at Ship Cove, and the ship sailed again on November 10. Cook's plan was to sail south to about

55 degrees and then west to Cape Horn. This distance was covered in five weeks, after which Cook wrote, "I have now done with the southern Pacific Ocean, and flatter myself that no one will think that I have left it unexplored."

The Southern Atlantic

The southern Atlantic, however, still remained. In early December, the *Resolution* reached Desolation Island off the coast of Chile—"The most desolate and barren country I ever saw," Cook wrote—and on December 29, it rounded the cape, leaving the Pacific behind. After a short rest at Staten Island, also known as Estados Island, to replenish their meat supply with fish, seals, penguins, and ducks, Cook and his crew headed southeast to 60 degrees and then east.

Cook did not expect to find anything of significance in the 5,000-mile journey to the tip of Africa, and he was correct. Clerke was initially hopeful that the first land they encountered might be part of a continent, but it was only an island, he wrote, as quoted by Hough, and "a very poor one, too." This did not stop Cook from landing, claiming it for England, and naming it the Isle of Georgia after King George.

Heading farther southeast, the *Resolution* came upon another island, the most southerly encountered, which Cook called Thule—a name used in ancient times to denote a place beyond the known boundaries of the world. A week later, he reached another group of islands, equally barren, which he named after Lord Sandwich. Three weeks later, nothing more having been discovered, the *Resolution* turned north for Africa, reaching Cape Town on March 21.

A few days earlier, Cook had learned from English sailors on a passing ship about what had happened to Furneaux's men at Grass Cove. "I shall make no reflections on this melancholy [sad] affair until I hear more about it," he wrote in his journal. "I shall only observe . . . that I have found them [the Maoris] no wickeder than other men."

The *Resolution* and her crew remained in Cape Town for five leisurely weeks. The last part of the mission was accomplished when Kendall's watch was checked against the known longitude of Cape Town. It was found to be accurate to within a third of a degree, a highly successful result.

The *Resolution* left Cape Town on April 27 and, after brief stops at St. Helena and the Ascension Islands (islands midway between South America and Africa) and a 1,500-mile detour to the island of Fernando de Noronha about 200 miles off the Brazilian coast, they reached England on July 29, 1775. The final entry in Cook's journal of the voyage demonstrates how much he cared for his men. "Having been absent from England three years and eighteen days," he wrote, "in which time . . . I lost but four men, and only one of them by sickness."

England, 1775–1776

WHEN JAMES COOK RETURNED FROM HIS FIRST VOYAGE, colleague Joseph Banks received most of the credit. At the end of his second voyage, there was no doubt in the minds of the Admiralty, the scientific community, the public, or even the king regarding whom to praise. It would have been the pinnacle of any explorer's career, and most people thought he was due well-deserved and honorable retirement. There were new discoveries on the horizon, however, and Cook was not ready to leave them to others.

Cook's arrival in London caused a stir among the Admiralty and the public. Lord Sandwich cut short a yacht cruise in order to offer his congratulations. Cook was promoted again, this time from commander to post captain, meaning that his name would be posted on a seniority list and that, should he live long enough, eventually he would become an admiral. His new commission was handed to him personally by King George. In return, Cook gave the king a collection of maps and charts.

The public's interest was fueled by reports in newspapers—largely fabricated in the absence of any official account from either Cook or from the navy. The *Morning Post* mistakenly referred to his ship as the *Endeavour* and claimed he had discovered "an island of vast extent. . . . The island, it is said, is inhabited by a race of people as singular in their manners as they are whimsical in their appearance." And *Lloyd's Evening Post* claimed to have heard directly from Cook about seeing "an amazing face of perpendicular rock" before he was blocked by Antarctic ice.

Such reports were by no means the extent of Cook's problems with accounts of his journeys—even his first one. At Cape Town, he had been made aware that his voyage on the *Endeavour* had been lumped with those of fellow English explorers Samuel Wallis, Philip Cartaret, and John Byron into a book by journalist John Hawkesworth.

Financed by Banks and authorized by Lord Sandwich, the book was a mishmash of truth and invention. Hawkesworth falsely claimed to have received the *Endeavour*'s journal directly from Cook and that Cook had helped edit the final manuscript of the book. Much of Cook's observations were attributed to Banks, and Banks even got credit for some of the drawings done by Parkinson and Buchan.

Cook had been worried about how to deal with Hawkesworth upon his return, but he found that the problem had taken care of itself. The book had been severely criticized by knowledgeable people, and Hawkesworth, his reputation ruined, had declined in health and had died while Cook was still in New Zealand.

Trouble with Förster

More trouble was just ahead, however, this time over the account of the second voyage. Johann Förster began pestering Cook, claiming the money he had been given for his work was

Cook gained much acclaim when he returned to England after his second voyage. He was made a Fellow of the Royal Society, awarded the Copley Gold Medal, and painted by notable portrait painter Nathaniel Dance-Holland. Above is the famous painting by Dance-Holland, which is now at the National Maritime Museum in Greenwich, England.

insufficient. He also claimed that Lord Sandwich had promised that he alone would be authorized to write a history of the voyage. Sandwich denied this, but he finally agreed that Förster would be allowed to publish, as a section of Cook's book, an account of scientific findings. When this was refused, Sandwich lost patience and decreed that Förster would not be allowed to write or publish anything. Förster ducked around this prohibition by writing under his son George's name, but Cook would never see this work, as it was published after he was at sea once more.

Such matters, however, were minor nuisances compared to the praise heaped upon Cook. His achievements, including putting to rest any notion of a great southern continent, led the Royal Society to elect him as a member. Significantly, his nomination was endorsed, not by the usual 3 or 4 members but by 25, including Solander, astronomers Nevil Maskelyne and Samuel Horsley, physicist Samuel Cavendish, and noted anatomist John Hunter. Also adding their signatures were Förster and Banks.

Even before landing in England, Cook had written to Banks, expressing his hope that the differences between them could be settled. This was accomplished so cordially that Banks insisted on commissioning a portrait of Cook. The portrait, done by Nathaniel Dance-Holland, shows Cook sitting in his naval uniform with a map spread before him. People who knew Cook personally said, at the time, that it was an excellent likeness.

The navy was proud of Cook, too. Lord Sandwich paid a personal visit to the *Resolution*, treated the officers to dinner, and approved the promotions Cook had recommended for Charles Clerke, Robert Cooper, and Isaac Smith. Moreover, the Admiralty was prepared to make Cook's financial future secure. He was appointed as one of the four captains at the Royal Navy Hospital, a position with few duties but which paid a handsome annual stipend, plus it provided comfortable quarters for families.

Another Expedition

Cook accepted the appointment with mixed feelings. He had learned within a short time of his homecoming that another exploratory voyage was planned, one that would address a dream almost as old as that of finding a southern continent. Europe's preferred routes to the Far East had been blocked—first the overland route was blocked by the Ottoman Turks' conquest of Constantinople in 1453, and then the sea route was blocked by Spanish and Portuguese domination of the Atlantic. Starting with a voyage by Englishman John Cabot in 1497, European nations had tried to find a "Northwest Passage" west, across the top of North America, and into the North Pacific. Another supposed passage was the Strait of Anian, which led east from what is now Alaska. It had appeared on fanciful maps ever since the New World was reached and partially mapped, but it had been the explorations of Denmark's Vitus Bering in 1741 that demonstrated that America and Asia were separated and that such a passageway might be possible.

Sometime in the months after Cook's return, he was told that the Admiralty was planning a two-pronged expedition to search for this passage. One ship would probe from the east in the Hudson and Baffin Bays, and the other would sail to the North Pacific and through the Bering Strait to search from the west.

The Admiralty thought—and so did Cook, at least for a time—that these expeditions would be commanded by others and that Cook's role would be that of an adviser. One of the ships headed for the Pacific would, indeed, be the *Resolution*, and Cook was consulted as to the other. Not surprisingly, he chose another Whitby-built vessel, whose name—the *Diligence*—was changed to the *Discovery*.

Fateful Dinner

The next most pressing question was that of who would command the two explorations. On January 9, 1776, Cook was invited to discuss these appointments over dinner at the Admiralty with Sandwich, Palliser, and Stephens. They quickly agreed that Cook's former lieutenant, Richard Pickersgill, would command the *Lyon* on the voyage to search westward from the Atlantic.

Several names were then considered for the Pacific voyage, among them Charles Clerke and John Gore. Both were experienced officers, but Cook was not sure they were ready for a command of this sort. According to Cook's first biographer, Andrew Kippis, as quoted by Beaglehole, Cook "was so fired [about the voyage] . . . that he started up, and declared that he himself would undertake the direction of the enterprise." The other three, who might well have been hoping for just such an outcome, were overjoyed, and Sandwich lost no time in telling the king.

In February, Cook wrote to Walker with the news, adding that he expected to sail toward the end of April. That would not be the case. Delay piled upon delay as the two ships were fitted out at the Deptford naval yard. Part of the problem was that Cook did not personally oversee the work as he had done with past voyages, this time being occupied with his portrait, his journals, and the dispute with Förster. As a result, Cook would not depart until mid-July, far too late to be able to reach the Arctic by the following summer. In addition, the ships were overhauled in a very slapdash manner, a fact that Cook would learn of, to his sorrow, shortly after sailing.

Selecting the Crew

Cook also was occupied with the selection of his officers and crew. His first lieutenant on the *Resolution* would be Gore, who had now been around the world three times and had gone with

Banks to Iceland. The fact that Gore's native America now was threatening to break away from Great Britain apparently had no effect on his willingness to serve in the British navy. In all, there would be seven Americans on the two ships.

The second lieutenant was James King. Although only 26, he had been in the navy since the age of 12 and, having studied science at Oxford, also could take on the duties of astronomer. In appointing John Williamson third lieutenant, Cook seems to have made a mistake. He was intelligent, but he had a violent temper and was thoroughly disliked by the crew.

The sailing master, William Bligh, had been recommended to Cook as an excellent navigator. Unfortunately, he also had an uneven temper, which would become much more pronounced when he later commanded the *Bounty*, whose men staged the famous mutiny.

Clerke was chosen to command the *Discovery*, with Jem Burney as his first lieutenant. Also of note were William Anderson, surgeon on the *Resolution*, and William Ellis, surgeon's mate on the *Discovery*, who was also a talented artist. Chief artist on the expedition was John Webber, whose work, when on display at London's Royal Academy, had attracted the attention of Solander, who recommended him to Cook.

Omai in England

The only other non-naval person on the voyage was Omai, the native of Huahine who had reached London with Furneaux aboard the *Adventure*. The Polynesian, with his quaint manners and exotic good looks, had become the toast of high society. Banks had taken a special interest in him, teaching him the basics of London drawing-room manners and dressing him in the latest fashions. He was introduced to everyone, even King George, to whom he said, as quoted by Hough, "How do, King Tosh!"

Omai had been in England almost a year before Cook arrived, however, and was beginning to wear out his welcome. The novelty had worn off, and Sandwich and Banks were more than ready for their guest to go home. The trip to take him there, then, was used as a cover story to disguise Cook's real mission, although it is difficult to think that any rival country would believe that the sole task of England's most famous explorer was to return a single Polynesian to his home island.

Not only was Cook to carry Omai to Huahine, but he was to take all his possessions as well. Included were furniture—a

OMAI IN LONDON

When Omai, the Polynesian taken aboard the *Adventure*, reached London, he became the toast of London society. Prominent hostesses vied with one another to have him at their parties, and he charmed nearly everyone he met.

One hostess thus charmed was the novelist Fanny Burney, whose brother Jem was one of Cook's officers. Her account of meeting him is quoted by Hough:

> He rose and made a very fine bow, and then seated himself again. . . . He had on a suit of Manchester velvet, lined with white sateen . . . lace ruffles, and a very handsome sword which the King had given to him. He is tall and very well made, much darker than I expected to see him, but has a pleasing countenance.

Burney also wrote, as quoted by Beaglehole, that Omai "seems to shame Education, for his manners are so extremely graceful, and he is so polite, attentive, and easy, that you would have thought he came from some foreign court."

feather bed, table, and chairs—along with kitchenware and china. There was port wine for his guests and a hand organ and jack-in-the-box to keep them entertained. For protection, he brought along muskets, gunpowder, and shot, plus a full suit of armor.

But Omai would have to give up his spacious cabin to make room for other passengers—the four-footed and winged kind. The king, who took such a keen interest in agriculture that many subjects called him "Farmer George," was convinced that the frequent tribal wars among the Tahitians would stop if only they were more productively employed. It was common to take livestock on long sea voyages to furnish eggs and fresh meat, but Cook was ordered to find room for, besides the normal compliment of animals, additional sheep and rabbits, four horses, hogs, a cow and bull, and even a pair of peacocks. In a rare moment of humor, Cook wrote to Lord Sandwich, as quoted by Maclean, that "Nothing is wanting but a few females of our own species to make the *Resolution* a complete ark."

There were more delays after Cook reached Plymouth, but the *Resolution* finally sailed on July 13. The *Discovery* remained behind. Its captain, Charles Clerke, was in a London prison because of debts owed by his brother. When finally released and aboard his ship, Clerke said, as quoted by Hough, "I shall get hold of him [Cook], I fear not." He confidently looked forward to the voyage, unaware that while in the dank, crowded prison, he had contracted tuberculosis.

Also confident was Cook's second lieutenant, James King, who noted in his journal that it was exactly four years since Cook had departed on his second expedition. Surely, he wrote, as quoted by Hough, this was "an omen of a like prosperous voyage."

The Third Voyage, 1776–1779

AFTER ONLY 11 MONTHS AT HOME, CAPTAIN JAMES COOK WAS off on another exploratory voyage. Once again he was looking for something long dreamed of, but this search would lead as far to the north as his others had led to the south. It would yield great discoveries but also great disappointments.

Cook's uncharacteristic lack of presailing oversight was felt immediately. Not only did the *Resolution*'s hull leak badly, but rain poured through gaps in the decking. The water spoiled so much of the livestock feed that the ship had to put in at Tenerife in the Canary Islands (off the northwest coast of Africa) for fresh supplies on the way to Cape Town.

On October 18, the *Resolution* reached Cape Town, where it was joined four weeks later by Clerke and the *Discovery*. Both ships needed extensive repairs, and it would be December 1 before they sailed again.

Plans called for New Zealand to be the next stop, but Cook used the opportunity to do a little exploring on the way.

He took a route far to the north of where his second voyage's route had sailed, traveling past and naming the Prince Edward Islands, passing the island found by and named for the French explorer Jules Crozet, and then stopping briefly at Kerguelen Island to celebrate Christmas.

With food for his livestock running low, Cook decided to stop first at Van Diemen's Land (see page 7). The ships anchored in Adventure Bay, where Furneaux had stopped on his way home two years earlier. During the four days in which they gathered wood, water, and grass, the crew was visited by Aborigines who seemed even more primitive than those they had encountered in Australia during the first voyage. A *Discovery* officer, John Rickman wrote, as quoted by Thomas, that they "seemed to live like the beasts of the forest in roving parties, without art of any kind."

Ten days later, Cook was at his familiar anchorage in Ship Cove. The Maoris seemed as apprehensive as they had been on the second voyage, but this time Cook knew why. They were afraid of reprisals from the Grass Cove massacre. Cook was careful, making sure every work party that went ashore was armed, but he finally convinced the Maoris of his friendship.

The Grass Cove Story

Eventually, Cook led a large party of five boats to Grass Cove. His purpose was to collect fodder for the animals, but also it was to see the scene of the bloodshed. At the cove, he met an acquaintance from the earlier voyages, a man he knew as Pedro. Pedro told him what had happened: The *Adventure*'s crewmen, directed by master's mate Jack Rowe, had paused in their work to eat a meal. Some of the Maoris with them stole part of their food and were beaten. The Maoris retaliated, and two were shot dead. But before Rowe's men could reload their muskets, they were overwhelmed, killed, and—in accordance with the Maori custom—eaten.

Cook now knew that the Europeans had been as much at fault as the Maoris and had overreacted in what should have been only a minor incident. Rowe had been known to have a bad temper, and he and his men may have been intoxicated, as well.

On February 25, after a stay of only 11 days, the expedition sailed from New Zealand. Before he left, however, Cook wrote about the often violent character of the Maoris: "It appears to me that the New Zealanders must live under perpetual apprehensions of being destroyed by each other; there being few of their tribes that have not, as they think, sustained wrongs from some other tribe, which they are continually upon the watch to revenge."

The *Resolution* and the *Discovery* sailed north, but they made little headway because of what Clerke, as quoted by Hough, described as "nasty light breezes." Cook, however, had no need to hurry. He was so far behind schedule that there would be no way to reach the Arctic during the summer, before it was iced in. The delay, however, made it necessary to find some spot to take on wood, water, and food for both the men and the livestock.

Food supplies were, indeed, running low—to the point where small amounts of food were being pilfered from the galley. When the crew declined to identify their guilty comrades, Cook took unusually and uncharacteristically harsh measures—the first of many on this voyage—cutting the crew's meat ration by a third. When the men then refused to eat any meat at all, Lieutenant King wrote, as quoted by Beaglehole, that Cook called it "a very mutinous proceeding."

Back to Tonga

In the continuing search for supplies, Cook decided to change his plan. He wrote that it was now too late "for me to think of doing anything there [the Arctic] this year." So, instead of

Due to the warm reception and consideration given to him and his crew, Cook named Tonga the Friendly Islands in 1773. Cook and his crew made several more visits to the Friendly Islands. The young islanders entertained the men with grand ceremonial dances (*above*), and boxing and wrestling matches.

continuing toward Tahiti, he swung west toward the Friendly Islands—Tonga—"where I was sure of being supplied with everything I wanted."

The ships reached the Tongan island of Nomuka in early May. The islanders furnished the needed supplies, but they also engaged in theft on an unusually active scale. They tried, wrote surgeon William Anderson, as quoted by Thomas, "to thieve every thing," even objects for which they had no apparent use. Again, Cook reacted harshly. He had seldom had natives flogged before, but now he did so, extending the punishment even to chiefs and sentencing one culprit to five dozen lashes, something Midshipman George Gilbert thought, as quoted by Hough, "rather unbecoming of a European."

When his business on Nomuka was done, Cook sailed—on the advice of a chief named Finau—to another island, Lifuka, which was reached on May 17. He and his men were entertained royally with feasts, boxing matches—although the Europeans were shocked at the matches between women—and dancing. Cook was especially enthralled by a dance featuring about 100 men flourishing canoe paddles. He wrote, "Such a performance would have met with universal applause on a European theatre."

Cook did not restrict himself to being only an observer of Tongan ceremonies. On July 8, an important chief named Paulaho invited him to what seemed to be a complex religious rite on the principal island of Tongatapu. But when Cook tried to walk to where it would be held, he was told that he could only watch, not participate. When Cook insisted, Paulaho relented, but only on the condition that the visitor strip to the waist and let his hair, bound with a ribbon, fall free. Cook did so, much to the discomfort of one officer, Lieutenant Williamson, who wrote, as quoted by Beaglehole, "I cannot help thinking he [Cook] rather let himself down."

Rampant Theft

Despite how hard Cook and his men tried to prevent it, theft on Tongatapu was just as prevalent as it had been on the other islands. Sometimes the islanders, when driven off, were so bold as to climb trees and throw coconuts and stones at the sailors. One of Cook's strategies was to seize the canoes belonging to a chief and threaten to destroy them if stolen goods were not returned.

Sometimes even this did not work, and then Cook took even harsher measures. He ordered some thieves not only to be severely flogged, but to have their ears cut off as a visible example to others. On one occasion, he marked a culprit by having crosses cut into his arms as deep as the bone. This, Gilbert wrote, as quoted by Beaglehole, "was an act I cannot account for any other ways than to have proceeded from a momentary fit of anger." Beaglehole also quotes William Bayly, the astronomer, as writing that Cook could "in some instances may be said to have been guilty of great cruelty."

On July 17, the expedition left the Friendly Islands and four weeks later was in Tahiti, landing at Vaitapiha Bay on the south side. When they had taken on food and water, the ships moved to the much better harbor at Matavia Bay. Cook already had given away some of his livestock in New Zealand and Tonga, but he now was able to rid himself of the rest, completing that part of his mission. He wrote that he felt himself "lightened of a very heavy burden; the trouble and vexation that attended the bringing of these animals thus far is hardly to be conceived."

The Tahitians welcomed the animals King George had sent and were awed by the horses, the first they had ever seen. When Cook and Clerke went riding, the islanders were so astonished that Cook thought it "gave them a better idea of the greatness of other nations than all the other things put together that had been carried amongst them."

Human Sacrifice

After a few days, Cook was fortunate enough to witness another Polynesian rite—a human sacrifice. A military leader, To'ofa, was preparing for battle and had killed a man to sacrifice to Oro, the war god. Cook, Anderson, and Webber, who drew the scene, were led near the *marae*, or temple, and asked to remove their hats. The dead man was in a canoe at the edge of the sea. After a long series of prayers and chants, during which one of

During his third voyage, Cook had the opportunity to witness many religious rites, including a human sacrifice while on Tahiti. It was common for a person of lower class to be killed as an offering to Oro, the god of war, before a battle with a neighboring tribal group.

the priests held two carefully wrapped and hidden figures of gods that had been brought from the *marae*, the corpse was brought from the canoe. Some hair and one eye were removed and given to the priests. Then, after more prayers, the man was taken inside the *marae* and buried.

The next day, To'ofa asked Cook what he'd thought of the ceremony. Cook answered that he disliked it and that he thought it would sooner bring defeat than victory. When Omai told To'ofa that, in England, a man committing a murder like that would be executed, the islander cried, as Cook wrote, "*Ma ino, ma ino*" or "Vile, vile!"

Trouble on Eimeo

In late September, Cook and his crew left a tearful Tahiti and sailed to nearby Eimeo, where more trading took place. There was trouble, however, over goats. Cook had obtained four in Tahiti, which had a small flock left there from previous voyages. A chief named Mahine had asked for a pair and had been refused; Cook wanted to save them for other islands. Shortly thereafter, one of the goats was stolen. No sooner had it been returned, the thief having been someone other than the chief, that a second goat was stolen.

Cook reacted with fury. Leading a group of about 40 men onto the island, he began burning houses and canoes. The next morning, he sent word to Mahine that unless the goat was returned, he later wrote, "I would not leave him a canoe in the island and that I would continue destroying till it came." He was as good as his word, breaking up and burning at least 18 canoes, each representing weeks of labor and also a great part of the owner's wealth.

Once more, his men were shocked. Gilbert wrote, as quoted by Hough, that Cook's actions "were so very different from his conduct in like cases on his former voyages." Even Cook sensed that he had gone too far, writing in his journal that the "unfortunate affair . . . could not be more regretted on the part of the natives than it was on mine." And King, as quoted by Thomas, accurately captured the relationship between the Europeans and those they "discovered," writing that "they may fear, but never love us."

Only one part of the mission to the Society Islands remained—the return of Omai. After anchoring off Huahine, Cook made arrangements for Omai to receive a piece of land with room for a house and a vegetable garden. The *Resolution*'s carpenters built the house—ironically using wood from the canoes smashed on Eimeo—and Omai unloaded all his many belongings. When the time for farewell came, Omai, with great dignity, shook the hands of all the officers with whom he had traveled so far. When he came to Cook, however, he broke into tears and threw his arms around his captain's neck.

Clerke and Anderson

There had been plans to leave two more men behind—Clerke and Anderson. Clerke had grown weaker, and Anderson quickly diagnosed his illness as tuberculosis, having recently made an identical diagnosis on himself. They knew they would have little time to live in the cold Arctic air, and they had asked Cook if they might remain behind in the warmth of the tropics, perhaps to enjoy more years of life. Cook agreed, but Clerke delayed so long in getting his charts and journal in order—perhaps because he was unwilling to abandon his captain—that when the *Resolution* and the *Discovery* headed north from the Society Islands on December 8, the pair were on board, knowing that their lives were now measured in months rather than in years.

Cook's orders were to sail to New Albion, the name given to the northwest coast of North America by Sir Francis Drake when he had visited there in 1579. He had claimed the territory for England, but no Englishman had been there since. Now, since England did not want to alert Spain to Cook's mission or to alarm Spanish settlements in California, the expedition was to sail due north from the Society Islands and then east to its destination.

Cook was sailing into unfamiliar waters, and it did not take him long to make a new discovery. It was an atoll, or a string of small islands surrounding a lagoon. Since the date was December 24, Cook named it Christmas Island and remained there a week, collecting about 300 green sea turtles, whose meat was highly prized.

The Hawaiian Islands

About two weeks later, on January 18, more land was spotted. This time it was "high land," or mountains, signifying a much greater landmass than an atoll. It was Oahu, one of the chain of islands Cook named after Lord Sandwich but that later reverted to its native name of Hawaii.

Bypassing Oahu, Cook headed for a second island, Kauai. He could see no suitable place to anchor, so he remained off the coast for a few days. The islanders hung back at first, but then they drew closer. Jem Burney, who had become fairly fluent in the language of the Society and Friendly Islands, shouted down to a canoe, asking the name of the island. To his astonishment, the people understood and answered. The Europeans shortly would discover that the Hawaiians, though slightly shorter and darker and with slightly different customs, were clearly Polynesian. Cook would marvel in his journal once more about how these people, using only canoes, had spread so far.

The ships eventually dropped anchor, however, and Cook led a party ashore. When he walked up onto the beach, several hundred people, to his great surprise, fell on their knees before him. He had never been shown such respect in his travels and did not know that he was being treated like the representative of a god.

He finally got the crowd to rise, and a brisk trade began. As was the case elsewhere in the Pacific, iron was highly prized, but it had a greater value than usual in Hawaii, where it was almost entirely unknown. Clerke wrote, as quoted by Hough, that a single nail "will supply my ship's company very plentifully with excellent pork for the day."

North America

The voyage resumed on February 2, and for a month there was no more land—and not even so much as a bird—to be seen. Then, on March 9, the American continent came into view. Cook had reached the coast of present-day Oregon, at about the same latitude as Salem. There was no way to land because of steady rain, heavy fog, and a strong west wind. Conditions were so adverse that Cook named the area Cape Foulweather, and it is still known as such today.

Farther north, he came to a latitude where Spanish geographers claimed there was a strait that had been discovered

EXPLORING NOOTKA SOUND

While in Nootka Sound off Vancouver Island, Cook, as he frequently did in other harbors, went on a short exploratory trip in a small boat rowed by his midshipmen. This particular trip was to locate a tree suitable for a new mast. According to one of the midshipmen, James Trevenen, as quoted by Beaglehole, such times gave Cook opportunities for moments of relaxation:

> We were fond of such excursions, although the labor of them was very great, as, not only this kind of duty, was more agreeable than the humdrum routine on board the ships, but as it gave us an opportunity of viewing the different people and countries ... Captain Cook also on these occasions, would sometimes relax from his almost constant severity of disposition, and condescend now and then, to converse familiarly with us. But it was only for this time. As soon as we entered the ships, he became again the despot [tyrant].

by Juan de Fuca in 1592. Cook did not see it and even wrote that there was little chance "that ever any such thing existed." For once, Cook was wrong. He had sailed past the strait, which separates Vancouver Island from the mainland, but on March 29, he managed to find a suitable harbor on the island's western shore—Nootka Sound.

The two ships were quickly surrounded by more than 30 canoes, which were much larger than any they had seen. The natives, wrote King, as quoted by Hough, had a "wild, savage appearance.... Their faces were daubed with red and black paint and grease, in no regular manner."

The expedition remained about a month, during which time the ships were recaulked and the sails were repaired. The natives—later identified as probably being members of the Nuu-chah-nulth nation—proved to be friendly, and considerable trading took place. Cook's men were glad to get thick, warm furs, and they marveled at the long log-constructed houses in which the natives lived in groups, as well as at the huge carved figures of animals, birds, and fish.

The journey got underway again on April 26, and by May 12 it had crossed latitude 60 degrees north and had found a protected refuge that Cook named Prince William Sound. Gore called the entrance Cape Hold-with-Hope, optimistic that it would lead into the Northwest Passage they sought. Bligh thought otherwise, and a short exploration showed him to be correct.

Despite's Gore's optimism, Cook was becoming less confident of finding a passage. The coast, instead of curving to the east, led northwest instead, and, after Prince William Sound, it even turned to the southwest. Cook's confidence returned, however, when a large opening came into view. He promptly named it Hope's Return, but Bligh again disagreed, telling Cook it was nothing more than a large river.

The site was promising enough, however, for Cook to spend 16 days there. He sent King and Bligh with two boats to see if it was, indeed, the strait they sought. They went as far as present-day Anchorage and discovered that it was, after all, only an inlet—today known as Cook's Inlet.

The Bering Sea

The month of June was spent going southwest—precisely the opposite direction of where they wanted to go. Cook came to the end of the Alaskan mainland and passed up what turned out to be the Unimak Passage. On June 26, he went in a thick fog through a much narrower and more dangerous passage— "Providence has conducted us through between these rocks where I should not have ventured in a clear day," he wrote—and into the Bering Sea.

The Bering Strait between North America and Asia was almost due north, but Cook had no way of knowing this. To continue his search for the Northwest Passage, he had to hug the western coast of Alaska, around Bristol and Kuskokwim Bays and Norton Sound.

On August 3, Anderson died. Cook wrote about him as "a sensible young man, an agreeable companion, well skilled in his profession." The next island on the horizon he named Anderson Island.

Six days later, the voyage reached the westernmost point of the Americas, named Cape Prince of Wales by Cook. When the ships tried to go through the Bering Strait into the Arctic Ocean, however, strong winds pushed them west to within sight of Asia. Finally, Cook was able to sail back east and through the Bering Strait. A week later, he could see brightness on the northern horizon that he knew to be ice. He named a nearby body of land Icy Cape, only about 150 miles southeast of Point Barrow, the northernmost point in Alaska. Later that day, at latitude 70°44'N (70 degrees, 44 minutes north), the *Resolution* and the *Discovery* came to a solid wall of ice and could go no farther.

A few days later, Cook wrote, "I did not think it consistent with prudence to make any farther attempts . . . so little was the prospect of succeeding." His thoughts now turned to the question of where to spend the winter.

Cook originally had planned to seek some Russian port, such as Kamchatka or Petropavlovsk, but that would have meant months of inactivity in an ice-bound port. He now knew of another place he could go, one that would allow him time for more exploration. On October 26, he headed south for Hawaii.

Kealakekua Bay, 1779

THEIR SEARCH FOR THE NORTHWEST PASSAGE BLOCKED BY ice, the *Resolution* and the *Discovery* spent most of November 1779 sailing south, away from the frozen north to the more hospitable climate of Hawaii. The natives, too, were hospitable, but that would change and bring tragedy.

On November 26, an island was spotted. Its position was so close to where he had been before that Cook knew it must be part of the same group, and so it was—Maui. Cook elected not to land, but he allowed Hawaiians to come aboard and trade as his ships cruised west along the northern coast of the island. As they rounded the northeast corner, another island came into view to the south, one far larger than the others in the group. One of the natives told Cook it was Owhyhee—Hawaii.

Approaching the northern point of the island, the crew could see natives on shore waving white cloths. Canoes raced out to meet them, white cloths streaming behind them. There was a brisk trade, but Cook could find no suitable place where the ships could land, as the shore was pounded by high surf.

Indeed, adverse winds and the lack of a harbor would keep the ships cruising along the northwest shore of the triangular island for seven weeks, alternately trading with canoe crews and getting blown far to the east. Not until December 12 did they round the eastern point at Cape Kumukahi.

On December 18, the ships rounded the island's southern point, Ka Lae. The western coast of Hawaii was much more promising, and on January 16, Cook at last found the harbor he sought at Kealakekua Bay. His ships were instantly encircled by hundreds of canoes. "I have nowhere in the sea

Pictured is a feather cloak, collected from Cook's third voyage. The most common color for Hawaiian ceremonial cloaks is a red background with yellow geometrical motifs and lower border. The red feathers are of the i'iwi bird and the yellow ones are of the o'o. Such a large cloak would have belonged to a man of high rank.

seen such a number of people assembled at one place," Cook wrote.

An old man, Koa the high priest, came aboard and conducted an elaborate ceremony during which Cook's shoulders were draped with a red cloth as the word *Orono* was repeated. Koa then indicated that Cook should come ashore for another ceremony. When Cook stepped onto the beach accompanied by Bayly and King, the thousands of people there fell to the ground whispering "Orono."

The priest led Cook to a stone *heiau*, or temple, where he was again wrapped in red cloth. Koa then led Cook to various images, pausing before a central figure, the only one wrapped in cloth. The priest knelt and kissed the cloth and indicated that Cook should do likewise, which he did. Then, after a feast, Cook returned to the *Resolution*.

Cook as "Orono"

Cook had no way of knowing that his ships had appeared off Hawaii precisely as the season of Orono, god of peace and prosperity in the Hawaiian religion, replaced that of Ku, the god of war. Orono was represented publicly by white tapa cloths carried on a stick, much resembling the white sails on Cook's ships. Furthermore, Orono was supposed to circle the island counterclockwise before coming to his temple—exactly as Cook had done. Cook was being worshipped, not exactly as a god, but as a god having taken human form.

A few days later, a huge double canoe approached the *Resolution*. In the rear sat a regal figure, resplendent in a feather cape, his face covered by a headdress. He indicated that Cook should come ashore with him. Once there, they entered a tent that had been set up to allow Bayly to make astronomical observations. The man removed his cloak, putting it around Cook's shoulders, then lifted his headdress to reveal himself as "Terryaboo," a chief they had entertained on board the ship at Oahu, who actually was Kalani'opu'u, king of all Hawaii.

The king had brought as a gift more feather capes and vast quantities of food. It was intended, although Cook could not have known it, as a final offering to Orono before the time came for the god to depart. As the days passed, the Hawaiians, while still friendly, became less respectful. Cook had made his last journal entry, but on February 2, King wrote, as quoted by Thomas, that the king "became inquisitive as to the time of our departing and seemed well pleased that it was to be soon."

Two days later, the anchors were hauled aboard, the sails were unfurled, and the ships were steered out to sea, accompanied by hundreds of canoes filled with people waving white cloths. Cook's intention was to visit some of the other islands, but a fierce storm split one of the *Resolution*'s masts. He had little choice but to return to Kealakekua Bay.

A Tentative Welcome

When the ships arrived, they were greeted by canoes, although not nearly as many as had been there before, but when it was clear that the ships meant to anchor, the canoes disappeared and the beach was deserted. After the crew put up a camp on shore as a headquarters for repair of the mast, wrote King, as quoted by Thomas, "very few of the natives came to see us."

On the morning of February 13, Kalani'opu'u arrived. He was puzzled. Orono had returned long before he was supposed to and from the wrong direction. The king asked why, and when he was told, wrote Jem Barney, as quoted by Hough, he "appeared much dissatisfied" with what he was told.

On February 13, passions boiled over when a native who stole tools from the *Discovery* was caught and beaten, and also when a fight broke out between islanders and members of the crew over the seizure of a canoe. When Cook learned of this brawl, as King wrote as quoted by Beaglehole, he said that he must now use force because "they [the Hawaiians] must not . . . imagine they have gained an advantage over us."

February 14

The night was peaceful, but the next morning Burney discovered that one of the *Discovery*'s small boats had been stolen from alongside it. Clerke told Cook, and the captain resolved to seize all the canoes and to hold them until his boat was returned. To prevent the canoes from being retrieved, he sent parties under the command of Bligh and Williamson to each end of the bay.

Cook went ashore with marine lieutenant Molesworth Phillips and nine of his men, who were all heavily armed. He had decided that instead of holding the canoes, he would make King Kalani'opu'u a hostage. They landed in a small cove of volcanic rocks near the village of Kaawaloa and headed directly for the king's house. Cook sent Phillips inside to tell Kalani'opu'u to come out. When he did, Cook took him by the hand and asked him to come to the ship.

The king appeared to agree and, with one of his sons on each side, made his way with Cook to the beach, the marines forming a wedge in front of them to separate the crowd. Two things then happened. First, a canoe landed with the news that a chief named Kalimu had been killed trying to slip out of the bay. Second, one of Kalani'opu'u's wives fell at his feet, begging him not to go aboard the ship.

Cook now abandoned his plan to take the king captive. He ordered Phillips to have his marines line up on the shore, facing the crowd. Phillips later wrote, as quoted by Beaglehole, that Cook said, "We can never think of compelling him to go on board without killing a number of these people."

The Death of Captain Cook

Three small boats were nearby—the one in which Cook had arrived, one commanded by Williamson, and one

This painting called *The Death of Captain James Cook* shows the quarrel that broke out on February 14, 1779. Cook and four of his men were killed. The crew got parts of their captain's body back, which they buried at sea.

commanded by William Layton. As Cook started toward them, a Hawaiian made as if to stab him with a dagger. Cook fired at him, but the barrel was loaded not with a ball but with a small shot, and the man was unharmed. Another man tried to stab Phillips, who fended him off. Cook fired his other barrel, this time killing a man, and then ordered his men to head for the boats.

Phillips then fired and his men joined in, but the Hawaiians, instead of scattering before the musket fire, charged the marines before they could reload. The marines scattered, scrambling over the rocks toward the boats. Phillips was stabbed in the shoulder and struck on the head by a stone, but he managed to reach safety, as did five of his men. Others were not so fortunate. Corporal John Thomas was stabbed in the stomach; he fell and did not get up. Three more marines went down and were cut to pieces.

Cook was now alone among the crowd. He walked slowly toward the water, hands behind his neck as if to protect himself from stones. A warrior came up from behind, hesitated, and then struck Cook on the head with a club. He fell on one knee and, before he could rise, was stabbed in the back of the neck by another Hawaiian. He fell into water about knee-deep, but he managed to get to his feet. He beckoned to one of the boats that was then just a few feet away, but then was once more clubbed on the head. He fell again, and this time he could not get up, the warriors swarming around him with knives and clubs.

The Aftermath

James Cook was dead. Both the Europeans in the boats and the Hawaiians on shore were shocked into silence. The Hawaiians fell back toward the village, and the boats took the survivors to the ships, not taking time to recover the bodies. Eventually, some pieces of the bodies of their murdered comrades were returned—the skull, some bones, and the hands, one of them easily recognizable by a distinctive scar. On February 22, wrote Clerke, as quoted by Hough, his crew "had the remains of Captain Cook committed to the deep, with all the attention and honour we could possibly pay it in this part of the world."

Many of Cook's men, Bligh the most outspoken, wanted to take wholesale revenge, killing every native and leveling every village. Clerke, now in command, would not allow it.

Nevertheless, what King described as "many reprehensible things," did occur: More than 30 Hawaiians were killed, and two had their heads cut off and displayed from the bow of one of the small boats.

At last, the Hawaiians and the Europeans reached something of a truce. Work on the *Resolution*'s mast was finished, and on February 23, the two ships departed from Hawaii, leaving their captain behind. Midshipman John Trevenen wrote, as quoted by Hough, that "a universal gloom and strong sentiments of grief were very observable."

Clerke was determined to continue the expedition. Accordingly, the two ships sailed north again and had no more luck than in the previous summer. Clerke himself finally would succumb to tuberculosis in August, and John Gore commanded the voyage to its end, reaching London on October 4, 1780.

Cook Remembered

News of Cook's death had preceded the *Resolution* by 10 months in letters Clerke had sent from Petropavlovsk. Lord Sandwich started a letter to Banks by writing, as quoted by Beaglehole, "What is uppermost in our mind always must come out first. Poor Captain Cook is no more." King George was reported to have wept at the news. He awarded a pension of £200 to Elizabeth Cook, who lived an additional 56 years, dying at the age of 94 having outlived not only her husband, but also all of her children.

Cook was hailed as the foremost sailor and navigator of his generation. When John Elliott, a midshipman on the first voyage, sat for his oral lieutenant's examination, the officers on the panel, hearing he had been with Cook, passed him with no further questions. Cook's explorations had brought fame, which he never really sought, and renown to his country. Poet William Cowper wrote:

When Cook—lamented, and with tears as just
As ever mingled with heroic dust;
Steer'd Britain's oak into a world unknown,
And in his country's glory sought his own.

And one of Cook's oldest friends, Palliser, built another monument at his own estate, praising him as:

Cool and deliberate in judging, sagacious in determining, active in executing, steady and persevering in enterprising, from vigilance and unremitting caution, unsubdued by labour, difficulties, and disappointments, fertile in expedience; never wanting presence of mind: always possessing himself and the full use of a sound understanding.

Perhaps Cook's greatest memorial was the respect and affection felt by his men. After his death, surgeon's mate David Samwell wrote, as quoted by Hough, "In every situation, he stood unrivaled and alone; on him all eyes were turned: he was our leading star, which at its setting left us involved in darkness and despair."

CHRONOLOGY

1728   James Cook born in Marton, England, on October 27.

1745   Cook is apprentice to shopkeeper William Sanderson in Staithes.

1746–1755   Cook begins as an apprentice, rises to rank of mate, in fleet of Whitby merchant John Walker.

1755   Cook volunteers as an ordinary seaman in Royal Navy on June 17.

TIMELINE

Cook volunteers as an ordinary seaman in Royal Navy on June 17

1728

1768

1755

James Cook born in Marton, England, on October 27

Cook promoted to lieutenant, leads voyage of exploration (August 26, 1768–July 13, 1771) to Tahiti, New Zealand, and Australia

1759	Cook involved in capture of Quebec on September 13.
1762	Cook marries Elizabeth Batts on December 21.
1763	Cook appointed surveyor of Newfoundland.
1768–1771	Cook promoted to lieutenant, leads voyage of exploration (August 26, 1768–July 13, 1771) to Tahiti, New Zealand, and Australia.
1772–1775	Cook leads second voyage (July 13, 1772–July 29, 1775) to the Antarctic, Tahiti, the Society Islands, New Zealand; promoted to post captain upon his return.
1776	Cook sets out on third voyage on June 25.
1779	Cook killed by Hawaiians on February 14.

Cook leads second voyage
to the Antarctic, Tahiti,
the Society Islands, New Zealand

Cook killed by Hawaiians
on February 14

1776

1772

1779

Cook sets out on third
voyage on June 25, 1776

GLOSSARY

BILIOUS   suffering from, caused by, or attended by trouble with the bile or liver

BRIG   a two-masted sailing ship that is square-rigged on both masts

COLLIER   a ship for carrying coal

FEINT   an attack aimed at one place or point merely as a distraction from the real place or point of attack

FODDER   food for domestic animals

LATITUDE   the distance on the earth's surface north or south from the equator

LONGITUDE   the distance east or west on the earth's surface, measured from the prime meridian at Greenwich, England

PALISADE   a fence of poles or stakes set firmly in the ground to form an enclosure for defense

PILFER   to steal, usually something small or of little value

PROW   the forepart of a ship or boat

QUININE   a white, bitter, water-soluble alkaloid used in medicine chiefly in the treatment of resistant forms of malaria

REEF   a ridge of rocks or sand, often of coral debris, at or near the surface of the water

REGIMEN   a regulated system

RENDEZVOUS   an agreement to meet at a certain place and/or time

SCHOONER   a sailing vessel having a foremast and mainmast, with or without other masts, and having fore-and-aft sails on all lower masts

STRAIT   a narrow passage of water connecting two larger bodies of water

WEIGH   in sailing, to raise the anchor

BIBLIOGRAPHY

Beaglehole, J. C. *The Life of Captain James Cook*. Stanford, Calif.: Stanford University Press, 1974.

———., ed. *The Journals of Captain James Cook on His Voyages of Discovery: Edited from the Original Manuscripts*. Cambridge, U.K.: Cambridge University Press for the Hakluyt Society, 1955.

Captain Cook Society. "Cook as a Commander—As His Naval Contemporaries Saw Him." Available online at *http://www.captaincooksociety.com/ccsu4197.htm*.

Finnis, Bill. *Captain James Cook: Seaman and Scientist*. London: Chaucer Press, 2003.

Hooker, Sir Joseph, ed. *Journal of the Right Hon. Sir Joseph Banks During Captain Cook's First Voyage in H.M.S.* Endeavour *in 1768–71 to Tierra del Fuego, Otahiti, New Zealand, Australia, the Dutch East Indies, Etc.* London: Macmillan & Company, 1896.

Hough, Richard. *Captain James Cook: A Biography*. New York: W.W. Norton & Company, 1995.

MacLean, Alistair. *Captain Cook*. Garden City, N.Y.: Doubleday, 1972.

Thomas, Nicholas. *Cook: The Extraordinary Voyages of Captain James Cook*. New York: Walker & Company, 2003.

FURTHER RESOURCES

Kratoville, Betty Lou. *Captain James Cook*. Novato, Calif.: High Noon Books, 2001.

Lawlor, Laurie. *Magnificent Voyage: An American Adventurer on Captain James Cook's Final Expedition*. New York: Holiday House, 2002.

Meltzer, Milton. *Captain James Cook: Three Times Around the World*. New York: Benchmark Books, 2001.

The Visual Dictionary of Ships and Sailing. London: Dorling Kindersley, 1991.

Warrick, Karen Clemens. *The Perilous Search for the Fabled Northwest Passage in American History*. Berkeley Heights, N.J.: Enslow, 2004.

WEB SITES

The Captain Cook Society
http://www.captaincooksociety.com
Dozens of articles on Cook, as well as numerous links to other sites.

LucidCafe: James Cook
http://www.lucidcafe.com/library/95oct/jcook.html
Interactive site with links to hundreds of Internet resources, recommendations for books, videos, and related products.

The Mariners' Museum—Age of Exploration: James Cook
http://www.mariner.org
Educational site sponsored by the largest international maritime history museum, filled with prized artifacts that celebrate the spirit of seafaring adventure.

Science @ NASA: James Cook and the Transit of Venus

http://science.nasa.gov/headlines/y2004/28may_cook.htm

Web sites used to encourage research and to help NASA scientists fulfill their outreach responsibilities. Tells the story of the transit of Venus from a historical perspective, namely from Cook's voyage to observe this scientific phenomenon.

PICTURE CREDITS

INDEX

ABOUT
THE AUTHOR

WILLIAM W. LACE is a native of Fort Worth, Texas, where he is executive assistant to the chancellor at Tarrant County College. He holds a bachelor's degree from Texas Christian University, a master's degree from East Texas State University, and a doctorate from the University of North Texas. Prior to joining Tarrant County College, he was director of the News Service at the University of Texas at Arlington and a sportswriter and columnist for the *Fort Worth Star-Telegram*. He has written 50 nonfiction books for young readers on subjects ranging from the atomic bomb to the Dallas Cowboys. He and his wife, Laura, a retired school librarian, live in Arlington, Texas, and have two children and four grandchildren.